Folklore
and the
Hebrew
Bible

Folklore and the Hebrew Bible

by
SUSAN NIDITCH

FORTRESS PRESS
Minneapolis

FOLKLORE AND THE HEBREW BIBLE

Scripture quotations, unless otherwise noted, are the author's translation.

The excerpt from *Folk Literature of the Gê Indians*, Vol. 2, ed. Johannes Wilbert
and Karin Simoneau (Los Angeles: UCLA Latin American Center Publications,
1984), is reprinted by permission of the publisher.

The excerpt from *Folk Literature of the Gê Indians*, Vol. 1, ed. Johannes Wilbert
and Karin Simoneau (Los Angeles: UCLA Latin American Center Publications,
1978), is reprinted by permission of the publisher.

The excerpt from *Folk Literature of the Bororo Indians*, Vol. 1, ed. Johannes Wilbert and Karin Simoneau (Los Angeles: UCLA Latin American Center Publications, 1983), is reprinted by permission of the publisher.

Library of Congress Cataloging-in-Publication Data
Niditch, Susan.
    Folklore and the Hebrew Bible / by Susan Niditch.
        p.   cm.
    Includes bibliographical references.
    ISBN 0-8006-2590-0 (alk. paper) :
    1. Folklore in the Bible.   2. Bible.   O.T.   Genesis III—
Criticism, interpretation, etc.   3. Bible.   O.T.   Exodus XII—
Criticism, interpretation, etc.   4. Bible.   O.T.—Parables.
I. Title.
BS625.N515   1993
221.6'6—dc20   93-17830
                                                                   CIP

Manufactured in the U.S.A.   AF 1-2590

97   96   95   94   93   1   2   3   4   5   6   7   8   9   10

Contents

Editor's Foreword

Folklore and the study of folklore have long been recognized as important for the interpretation of the Hebrew Scriptures. In the last decades of the nineteenth century, when the folklore of various cultures was being collected and classified, Hermann Gunkel brought the work of folklorists such as the Grimm brothers into the service of biblical studies. Not only did Gunkel recognize that the Hebrew Scriptures preserve many folk tales and other folk literature, he also demonstrated how knowledge of the development of folk literature could be applied to the analysis of the Bible. In particular, he stressed the importance of the oral tradition—a key feature of a great deal of folklore—in the growth of Hebrew literature.

In the last few decades, as Susan Niditch demonstrates, there has been a virtual explosion in application of folklore studies to the interpretation of the Hebrew Bible. Issues such as the power and limits of the oral tradition, the difficulty of distinguishing between oral and written transmission, the poetic and aesthetic features of folklore, and the relation of folklore to folk practice and performance have come to the fore.

It is not easy to define folklore, but efforts to do so often shed light on biblical texts and the biblical world. As Professor Niditch points out in this volume, "folklore" is both the material that is studied and the name of the discipline—better, disciplines—that carry out such study. Folklore itself has generally been understood as tales, songs, sayings, and the like that arise and are passed on orally among a people. Earlier scholars tended to understand folk literature as that which cannot be attributed to a particular author. But on several counts such an understanding is insufficient. On the one hand, folklore is by no means limited to literary or verbal traditions but includes practices such as dances, music, rituals, and celebrations. On the other hand, although oral transmission among a culture is characteristic of folklore, "authors" or originators may be known.

As Professor Niditch shows in this volume, the discipline of folklore is actually an interdisciplinary enterprise. On the one hand, the recognition of the importance of folklore and the study of it have contributions to make to other approaches to biblical texts and to the study of the biblical world. To overlook folklore is to miss important facets of biblical literature and culture. On the other hand, the study of folklore intersects with other disciplines, such as form criticism, redaction criticism, tradition history, contemporary modes of literary criticism, and feminist interpretations.

This volume is designed to introduce the student of the Hebrew Bible to some of the rich possibilities of contemporary folklore study. It does so first by bringing the reader into the conversation among folklorists, both within and beyond biblical studies, and then by means of the investigation of a range of exemplary texts.

—Gene M. Tucker
Emory University

Acknowledgments

I want to thank my students at Amherst College and my teachers at Harvard University for their many contributions to my thinking about folklore and the Bible over the last twenty years. This book is dedicated, in particular, to the memory of Albert B. Lord, a brilliant scholar and generous teacher. I am grateful to have been among his students.

My work in chapter 3 has no doubt been influenced by the students in my course "Folklore and the Bible," one of whom, Lisa Gelber, expanded an assignment in that course into a senior honors thesis on the Passover Seder in Jewish traditions. This chapter was also shared with the members of the Colloquium for Biblical Research who met in Richmond, Virginia in August 1992. I thank the members for their most helpful comments and criticism. I also thank James Crenshaw and Dan Ben-Amos for their excellent suggestions concerning chapter 4.

The entire work has been read with his usual care by Gene Tucker, the editor of the series to which this book belongs. I thank him for his patience and intelligent assistance. I also thank my husband, Robert Doran, for reading every word, for always remembering obscure but relevant bibliographic details, and for helping me with everything in life, academic and non-academic.

Introduction

However—and the reader will have certainly long since asked the question—what has the Bible to do with folktales? Is it not an attack on the prestige of the holy book to see in it products of the imagination? And how can the lofty religion of Israel—to say nothing of the New Testament—contain material filled with what may be creative, yet nevertheless entirely subordinate, belief? These questions must be answered, first by saying that the Bible hardly contains a folktale anywhere. The elevated and rigorous spirit of biblical religion tolerated the folktale as such at almost no point and this near total eradication from the holy tradition is one of the great acts of biblical religion.

Gunkel 1987:33

The Bible is not traditional literature, but sophisticated, refined literature written down to cope with the traditional literature, and to make it appropriate for its "Sitz im Buch" in Scripture.

Zakovitch 1991:235

The words of Gunkel—who was perhaps the most "folkloristically" aware Bible scholar of his time, like those of Zakovitch, a modern scholar with genuine interests in traditional literatures and folklore scholarship, admit of discomfort in equating or associating folklore with the Bible. While Gunkel portrays biblical writers as censors, Zakovitch sketches them in his own image, scholars in their studies, poring over written manuscripts, editing and elaborating in accordance with certain theological assumptions. Zakovitch says overtly what Gunkel implies—

that "traditional literature" is primitive, unrefined, and unsophisticated—something the Bible cannot be.

As a whole, modern scholarship is still hampered by the discomfort or embarrassment manifested in Gunkel's apologetics and Zakovitch's disclaimers, although there are brighter signs. In the last decade the field of folklore studies has gained a new acceptance among contemporary biblical scholars. Works by Sasson, Culley, Fontaine, Hendel, Kirkpatrick, Milne, myself, and others testify to this renewal of interest as does the recent translation into English of Hermann Gunkel's classic study of *The Folktale in the Old Testament*. And yet, introductory texts to biblical literature and the courses that introduce most undergraduate and divinity students to the field of Hebrew Scriptures still tend to neglect folklore, emphasizing instead ancient Near Eastern backgrounds, archaeology, history, and traditional source-critical, redaction-critical, and form-critical approaches to the literature. Advanced courses add philological, text-critical, and epigraphic tools to the skills necessary for the study of Israelite history and literature, but folklore studies generally are not included as a regular part of introductory or advanced work.

In fact, Robert Alter's recently expressed preference for interpreting the Bible "without folklore" (1990), based on a lack of understanding of what folklore is—folklore, the rich corpus of material to be studied and folklore the complex and intellectually stimulating interdisciplinary field of inquiry.

One goal of the present work is to introduce folklore, the field of study and the sorts of primary material often included under the rubric. This is no simple task, for folklorists themselves engage in lively debates concerning the nature of their discipline and the definition of folklore itself (Ben-Amos, 1972; 1976b; and articles in Dundes, 1965c:4–51).

After exploring some of the major issues and threads in contemporary folklore studies, I will provide a series of case studies, applying some of the methodologies introduced in chapter 1 to passages and problems in Scripture. How does the study of folklore enrich and alter our study of the Bible by raising new questions or setting the old ones in new light? How can the methodologies of folklore join source criticism, form criticism, redaction criticism, tradition history, and composition criticism as a tool of biblical studies—the goal of all these methodological approaches being a deeper understanding of biblical literature, its creators, and their worldviews.

1
The Field of Folklore

DEFINING FOLKLORE

Many modern folklorists consider true folklore to be lore in process or performance (Ben-Amos, 1972:9; Toelken:38). The "lore" would include narrative forms such as folktales, oral histories, legends, myths, and ballads; verbal interactive forms such as proverbs, riddles, and jokes; dramatic, play-acting forms such as rituals and children's games; and various forms of material culture such as handmade quilts and other varieties of folk art.

The terms "process" and "performance" imply the work's living currency in a social context, during its very creation and in the experience of those who share in its becoming. The "folk group" receives the piece of folklore or interacts with it in an ongoing culturally defined and expressed relationship between creative artists and appreciative audiences, who actually influence the creative process itself (Bauman, 1986a:2). Thus folklore would include a Native American's rendition of tales of Coyote trickster, his own version of an ancient northwest American tradition of storytelling; a Vermont grandma's quilt, patterned with her own creative variations on the quilting themes of previous generations; or jokes current among teenagers in Detroit who constitute a folk group with its own sociolinguistic identity, its own social context.

This is a very dynamic definition of folklore with implicit emphases on the folklorist's observation of the creative process, the direct recording of verbal genres, and the contemporary existence of the folk groups for whom the lore is meaningful. It leads a modern collector like Dennis Tedlock to seek new ways of recording and preserving the tales he collects to provide a record not only of words and context but of the very nuances of the narrator's voice, the caesuras, and the gestures (1983:3–19 and

3

throughout; 1990). Such a definition unnuanced, however, runs the risk of failing to take full account of another feature of folklore—tradition.

The Native American's performance of tales of Coyote is one in a lengthy tradition of storytelling among his people and represents his creative participation in plots, characterizations, and styles of narration that have many precursors and ancient roots. But are nineteenth-century versions of such tales examples of folklore? These texts were collected by people not attuned to scientific methods, who had none of the recording technology available to the modern collector. The narrators are dead, their immediate folk groups are gone, their cultures in nineteenth-century forms have disappeared and what remains are transcripts. Do the Grimm tales qualify as folklore, given that they were purposefully contoured (Ellis would say virtually "forged" [1983:viii]) before publication by their collectors, the Grimm brothers (see Rölleke; Zipes, 1988:13–15, 113–14; Bottigheimer, 1991; Ellis:37–71)? What then of archaic works such as Homer's *Odyssey* or the many seemingly traditional works of the Hebrew Bible? What of prophetic sign acts—dramatic stylized forms of expression that appear to be performances? Accounts of such performances have been shaped by a literary process and placed in larger narrative contexts that lend them meaning. Are they examples of folklore?

Some scholars would exclude the works of the Bible from that which is folklore. Dan Ben-Amos writes of the biblical writers' ideological biases, the ways in which they "flatten out" and recast what was oral folklore into written stories that are theologically acceptable and uniform (1990:37, 42). Folklore is relevant to the Bible only in what it elucidates about the process of moving from oral to written literature. Ben-Amos's point seems especially relevant when exploring a work such as Proverbs. The biblical book of Proverbs does not present "live" sayings in context but is a bookish collection in which groups of sayings create and find a new bookish context.

ORAL COMPOSITION

The issue of oral versus written is an important one in defining folklore, and one that relates to questions about the nature of biblical material in complex ways. And yet a definition limiting folklore to what is observably "lore in process" is too restrictive and leads unnecessarily to a view of Scripture as dead literature, a mere shadow of what may have once been "real" lore. In contrast to a host of modern folklorists whose list includes Toelken, Bauman, and Ben-Amos, another group including Albert Lord,

David Bynum, John Foley and many other Lord-trained students do consider the ancient Greek, Anglo-Saxon, and Celtic works they study to be examples of narrative folklore, because they believe they are able to demonstrate that this material is rooted in material that was orally composed. This literature reflects or was derived from lore performed and in process. The relationship between lore in process and oral-derived works in any cultural trajectory is a topic of debate and discussion among scholars. Is the Greek *Iliad*, for example, a transcription of an actual performance, is it based upon many oral performances familiar to a traditionally versed writer, is it a work written by an author able to use oral-formulaic language as if he were a bard (see Foley's discussion 1992:294–98)? Whatever the answers to these elusive questions, the dynamic, living quality of works such as the *Iliad* is enshrined in the very nature of their formulaic language revealing how artists of particular cultures shared certain ways to describe certain images or ideas and freshly improvised on formulaic patterns of speech within certain metric conventions. These tales of heroes, victories, journeys, and families follow certain patterns of content which are as formulaic and yet as richly renewable and open to variation as the language in which they are expressed. The repetitions in content and language are not, as Lord has noted, merely a means of providing ready-made lines for a storyteller who has to think on his feet or a means of reminding an illiterate audience, who has no script, of essential contours of plot and characterization but rather a means of emphasizing and projecting key aspects of culture and worldview. Repetitions in language and content reveal the thoughts and concerns that are at the conceptual heart of the tradition (1987:58). For students of oral literature such as Lord, as for Bauman, Ben-Amos, and other contemporary folklorists, these narrative traditions are expressions of particular cultures and times. Lord reminds us, however, that the folk productions of a culture at any one time rest on the folk productions of earlier tellers and spinners (1987:62; Bynum, 1976:55) and that there is an even wider conceptual realm to which they belong having to do with our very nature as people (Bynum, 1990:70). As scholars from wide-ranging fields (von Hahn, Rank, Campbell) have noticed, tales of heroes such as Odysseus or Gawain have much in common with narrative patterns of other tale-telling traditions, all of which can shed light on one another. This statement is true also of other folk narrative patterns and other folk genres. Many reasons for cross-cultural similarities in the structure and content of folk materials have been offered ranging from Jung's emphasis on inborn archetypal images out of which people construct both unconscious dreams and conscious imaginings in narrative to Aarne and Thompson's suggestions that stories begin at one geographic location from which they spread (see below, pp. 15–18). Lord and his school allow folklore its universal and specific aspects. They stress the appreciation of ancient cultures through the ancient lore, and lead one to speculate upon the ways in which many cultures and humans may constitute a macro "folk group" of sorts if one explores for some of the recurring patterns and content shared by works of folklore.

THE BIBLE AND ORAL COMPOSITION

Can biblical literature qualify as folklore with this more antiquarian approach to performance in the past? Robert Culley's excellent review article (1986:30–65) carefully and thoroughly presents discussions since the last century concerning possible oral roots of biblical literature. Early twentieth-century scholars such as Gunkel and modern ones such as Claus Westermann assume, like Ben-Amos, the existence of oral tellings behind written and reshaped biblical accounts, and are sensitive to what they regard as qualities of oral-style narration that remain identifiable within the written texts. Other scholars such as Culley (1967), Urbrock (1972; 1975; 1976), and Whallon (1963; 1969) have carefully explored biblical poetic texts to see if oral-formulaic style lies behind the parallel pairs and the larger recurring syntactic and lexical patterns of biblical prosody. I have speculated on the possibility that prophets delivered their oracles extemporaneously, building their verses of doom or salvation and combining them to create image units and literary forms such as the "woe oracle" or the "lawsuit" (Niditch, 1980a). Burke Long (1976a; 1976b), David Gunn (1974a; 1974b; 1976), and Robert Doran and I (1977) have explored the patterns of content in biblical narrative, pointing to the repetitions, the economy of plot, the typological role of characters, and the way in which the narrative patterns evoke those of the traditional or orally composed literatures of other cultures. Others such as Carole Fontaine (1982) and Claudia Camp (1990) have speculated about possible performance roles of "wise women" mentioned in the Hebrew Scriptures or the live in-context use made of proverbs in ancient Israel. However, all of us who have worked in this area agree that one can never truly know whether or not individual pieces of Israelite literature were orally composed or based on oral compositions, nor can one reconstruct with certainty the social contexts so essential to understanding folk genres as oral performance and interaction. We know too little about the education process

6

that might have produced wise women or the means by which prophets acquired and passed on their poetic skills or if ancient Israel had its own traditions of "singers of tales." The sample of poetic texts is too small to allow one to test for oral-formulaic composition in the style of the scholarship of Lord (1968). And yet even given these demurs, much is to be learned by treating the Bible as folklore.

TOO MUCH EMPHASIS ON ORAL COMPOSITION?

Enthusiasm in search of the Bible's oral roots in some ways has led scholars astray, blinding them to the full potential of using folklore, the field, and comparative folk materials to explore the traditional literature of the Hebrew Bible as it now stands. Although Gunkel and Westermann certainly enrich our reading by drawing upon folk materials in their studies of Genesis, they see supposed traits of "orality," of what was once oral, as a means of demarcating early biblical material or of tracing the diachronic history of a literary tradition (see also Van Seters, 1975:183). Ben-Amos (1990) is interested in this process as well. In this way, folklore for the biblical scholar becomes a branch of redaction criticism or tradition history. But as noted above it is not possible to prove that any biblical work was orally composed. And even if it were possible to do so, a written version of a story could be earlier than a later singer's oral version. In short, to ask if a piece of Scripture was orally composed may not be the most important question. Here we arrive at the interesting and important issues concerning the relationship between oral and written works and the relevance of a contrast between "oral" and "written" for defining folklore and for exploring the relevance of folklore to the Hebrew Bible.

Some scholars have strongly demarcated between oral and written compositions and between the cultural and intellectual assumptions behind them. Walter Ong and his disciple in New Testament studies, Werner Kelber, have done much to perpetuate an image of the "great divide" between oral and written literatures and between oral and written worldviews. The anthropologist Jack Goody adds fuel to the contention that oral and written are different ways of approaching and understanding the world. Even while stating clearly that he rejects romantic portraits of the noble savage (1987:293), Goody finds the writing mode to be "more reflective" than the oral mode (1987:293) and concludes dramatically that "writing underpins civilization." (1987:300) To his credit, Goody insists that the "primitive" mind does not differ from ours (1977:12), that any human society has intellectual activity and "even intellectuals" (1977:35), and he denies being an adherent of the "great divide" theory (1977:35). But in exploring his central theory that tremendous "new potentialities for human cognition are created by the introduction of writing" (1977:17) he ends up making rather sweeping generalizations of his own about oral and written worldviews. In particular, Ong draws a contrast between pre-literate cultures and literate ones, between literatures and modes of thought that are "aggregative" rather than "analytic," "redundant" rather than "sparse", "empathetic" and "participatory" rather than "objectively distanced," "situational" rather than "abstract" (see Ong, 1982b:37–57 and Lord on Ong, 1987:54–72). He stresses a difference between the pristine genuineness and immediacy of oral tradition versus the artificiality and removed, secondary quality of the written (1982a:10–21; 1982b:45–46). In spite of his genuine respect for each mode of thought, Ong ends up painting a portrait of the noble, illiterate savage, limited in terms of rationality, logic, and historical consciousness, but free, immediate, un-alienated, and at home in his context. If the definition of folklore has to do with an oral mentality described by Ong, then it is appropriate to ask Gunkel's question, "What does the Bible have to do with folklore?"

Albert Lord, albeit in a most diplomatic way, shows that Ong's characterization of oral literatures is almost amateurish: oral compositions can be extremely complex and long, philosophically sophisticated (see also Finnegan, 1970:21; 1988:45–58). Formulas are not merely to aid illiterates in remembering simple stories but have significance for worldview in shaping and reflecting meanings and messages. Brian Street's seminal study has, I believe, put to rest these theories of the great divide by showing that ultimately humans are humans with the same working parts. The characteristics of a society and the nature of its ideology, which develop in response to a wide range of economic, social, political, and ecological factors, affect attitudes to literacy but literacy itself does not transform people into becoming "more rational" or make them look at the world differently than those who read and write (Street:117).

While Lord's early work emphasized that the culture must be nonliterate for oral composition to take place, his recent comments have been much more nuanced. We have come to realize that "oral and literate societies exist in a continuity, not in a dichotomy, as do their lyrics and narratives." (Rosenberg:74) Ruth Finnegan's research has shown that there is no simple evolution in societies from oral to written, but rather feedback between the two throughout a culture's history (1970:16–19; 1982:23–25). In the Pacific cultures she cites, written materials become the sources for oral compositions, which are then written down, becoming available to authors who then create new oral works based upon them (1982:22–33). She cites Salmond's reference to the little notebooks used by Maori orators in New Zealand containing "random jottings [on] . . . genealogies . . . and . . . fine turns of phrases for future use (1982:23–25; 1988:111; see also 1974:56–57). Are the compositions that emerge less traditional, folkloristic, or oral for having been assisted by written notes? Contributors to *Text and Tradition* (ed. Niditch) show how the written biblical text is "reoralized" in Jewish midrashic tradition, which is itself written down in classical and medieval times and reoralized again in modern Jewish folklore. Moreover, William Graham has explored "the oral dimension of written scriptural texts, the ongoing function of scriptural texts as oral phenomena." (1987:7, 155–57, 171, see also Finnegan, 1970:18) This feedback between oral and written surely functioned throughout the biblical period and helped to shape Scripture just as the Bible's tones, textures, rhythms, language, narrative content, and structures have helped to shape subsequent oral and written traditions. What is important ultimately in describing and appreciating folk literature is not a question of oral versus written, but a matter of how traditional the work is in form and function (Lord in Niditch, 1990:2). And here we find a large spectrum.

DEFINING THE "TRADITIONAL": THE SPECTRUM

Rather than define folklore as orally based, I will describe it in terms of "the traditional." (See Foley's relevant comments on "register" [1992:286–89].) One salient trait of traditional literature is patterned repetition. The repetition takes many forms as symbols, words, syntax, elements of content, structures, and thoughts recur in a profound economy of expression and density of emphasis.

A single narrative work, such as the story of Rebecca and Jacob's theft of Esau's blessing in Genesis 27, is framed by Isaac's words to Esau, overheard by Rebecca, reported to Jacob, and acted upon (27:3,4; 27:7; 27:9; 27:14,17). Words and images of eating and blessing recur (27:25,31,33) signaling the importance of what is being stolen and the means by which the trick is achieved. The old man's simple desire for food and his eldest son's honest and ready interest in securing it for him, thereafter to receive his rightful blessing, contrast with the mother and younger son's wily use of provisions to achieve hidden goals, namely to obtain a status that the order of Jacob's birth should not allow.

9

In a traditional literary culture, moreover, certain types of stories recur, as do small narrative patterns, the building blocks of larger narratives that Lord calls "themes." Thus the story of Joseph's rise at court through the interpretation of dreams (Genesis 41), finds a parallel in Daniel's success as court wise man in Daniel 2. The tale of the patriarch who tells the foreign ruler his wife is his sister finds variants in Gen 12:1–10; 20; and 26:1–18. Jacob's rivalry with Joseph finds echoes in the implicit rivalry between Ishmael and Isaac and Ephraim and Manasseh and the explicit rivalries between Cain and Abel, Joseph and his brothers, and Leah and Rachel. Such repetitions in patterns of content are not confined to narrative traditions in the ancient Israelite narrative corpus. The prophetic woe oracle always includes the element "Woe to," the object of the woe word, and the explanation of the condemnation, often included in the descriptive object itself. Such oracles are found in Isa 1:4–9; 5:11–13,18–23; Am 6:1–8; and Hab 2:15–17. Similarly, the symbolic vision form includes a description of the seen object, a question about its significance, and an interpretation (Am 7:7–9; 8:1–3; Jer 1:11–12; 24; Zech 1–6; Dan 7–8). The form changes over time and each prophet/artist employs it with his own creativity and in response to the needs of his audience and the tastes of his times, all under the heading of what he perceives to be God's message through him, but the form has remarkable stability through time and is a set pattern available to the prophet with a particular sort of message. This is the nature of traditional-style composition.

The repeating themes, forms, and stories evidence the sort of repetition in language to express a given idea, image, or piece of content that is found in an individual traditional narrative such as Genesis 27 or Genesis 12. When the ruler in Genesis 41 and Daniel 2 is unable to solve his difficult problem, to uncover the meaning of his dream, he calls to a chain of court wise men. The verb "call to," *qr' l*, is followed by a chain of terms for court members (Gen 41:8; Dan 2:2). Variations on this formula are found elsewhere in Scripture (see also Ex 7:11). There is a way in Israelite narrative tradition to refer to court wise men and their summoning, and as noted above the phrase is not the rote, exact repetition one would expect of a copier of one version of the tale, but a recognizable variation on a particular formula pattern. Other examples are the reward formula pattern in Gen 41:40 and Dan 2:48 and in prophetic texts the varying uses of formula patterns in Isa 1:11, Am 5:22, Isa 1:14, and Am 5:21.

Finally, certain folk forms recur cross-culturally. Hence the possibility of Aarne-Thompson's massive international classificatory collection of folktale plots called types, and of smaller narrative building blocks called

10

motifs. Much is to be criticized in these systems of classification and in the way they define "the type" and "the motif" (see pp. 15–18) but the fact remains that there are many stories in the world like Genesis 41 and Daniel 2 about the unlikely hero of low status who raises his status by being the only one able to solve a conundrum posed by a person of higher status (type 922). The version of this type found in ancient Israel is culture bound; the specific versions in Daniel 2 or Genesis 41 are bound by their own more specific contexts and authorships. But once recognized, the link with a larger fund of lore is apparent and enormously instructive in coming to appreciate the underlying forms, meaning, and messages of these particular tellings of the tale. Cross-cultural comparisons reveal what is unique and what is not.

It has been argued that certain folk genres, such as the riddle, are evidenced all over the world, identifiable by their morphology (Georges and Dundes, 1963), while it can easily be shown that certain proverbs in form and/or content find parallels beyond their own cultural context (Fontaine, 1982). As Ben-Amos cautions, however, we must always be attuned to the ways in which cultures or smaller folk groups themselves define folk materials (1976a). The analysis of the use of the term *mashal*, for example, will be an interesting exercise in our chapter on wisdom. *Mashal*, sometimes translated as "proverb," appears to comprise a much wider category that includes what we call "proverb" as well as other sorts of material as well (see Finnegan, 1970:390–93). Many cultures do not distinguish between myth, folktale, legend, and epic. If the ancient Israelites did not do so, it may be artificial for us to do so. We are certainly taking liberties and being inaccurate when writing of "legends of Genesis" or the "patriarchal sagas" or the "exodus epic." For a detailed critique of Westermann's use of André Jolles's European categories and Albert de Pury's use of those of the folklorist Erich von Sydow, see Niditch, 1987:7–8; Kirkpatrick:41–42. Nevertheless when used with caution, comparative work can be helpful. The sharing of patterns and motifs found in various cultures is itself a trait of folklore—a trait evidenced by the Bible.

The presence of repetition in its various forms within a tradition implies a certain *Sitz im Leben*—not the romantic, pastoral, shepherd image of Gunkel nor the equally romantic I-thou oral world of Ong, but a setting in which for example there are certain ways in which prophets chastise a king or berate a faithless people; ways in which an author develops the success story of an unlikely hero; ways in which battles are described and enemies said to be subdued; situations that call for proverbs and certain patterns of speech underlying the proverbs quoted. These "ways" involve conventions of expression and imagery, recurring combinations of words and content into always fresh and varying but recognizable and familiar combinations. Notions of performance concerned with authors/creators and audiences/receivers underlie this way of looking at folklore and the Bible, but one need not assume that the traditional forms of the Hebrew Bible were orally and extemporaneously performed. Rather these forms are imbued with that quality of the traditional that always characterizes what is observably oral performance but that also characterizes material created in the traditional mode, a way of producing literary art that involves internalization of this particular poetic, rhetoric, or aesthetic, assumptions and expectations about what makes for and contributes to the tradition on the part of producers and recipients of the lore.

Not all biblical literature is equally traditional in this sense, nor is all modern written material equally nontraditional. There is a spectrum (see Finnegan, 1970:18,20,25.) The Genesis 12 version of the tale of the patriarch who tells the foreign ruler that his wife is his sister is more traditional than the version in Genesis 20 (Niditch, 1987:29–39). J. R. R. Tolkien's novels are more traditional in style than those of Faulkner. In modern America, the soap opera is a popular mode with stock characters, recurring narrative patterns, clear conventions, and audience expectations as was the gothic novel in nineteenth-century England. These works lie closer to the traditional than the film "Out of Africa" or a Walt Whitman poem. All artistic works adhere to conventions of some sort, are based on previous compositions, and are grounded in particular cultural and artistic contexts but the more innovative they are, the less they have in common with a range of comparable works—even allowing for each author's own voice and muse—the less traditional they are. As with all literary criticism, the analysis of context and form is at the heart of folklore methodologies dealing with questions of defining, describing, and classifying the varieties of folklore.

STRUCTURE AND CONTENT: TOOLS AND METHODOLOGIES

How does one describe and understand the building blocks of any one piece of folklore? How are the components—words, content, the patterns of meaning they create—related to one another in a work? How does the integrated piece, filled with content and patterned in certain ways parallel such combinations elsewhere—in a single tradition or cross-culturally—to constitute a genre? What is the significance of structure and content for understanding a work's composition and transmission history? These questions are central to the critical study of the prose and poetry of the Bible, and evoke aspects of form criticism, redaction criticism, and the study of tradition history.

Perhaps the dominant aspect of folklore is narration. Even a proverb sets a scene or tells a brief illustrative story. A riddle, in some sense, is an unfinished story that challenges the listener to complete it properly. A piece of decorative art sends a message of boldness and assertion, or beauty and delight—a story lies behind it and emerges from it—depending upon the colors, symbols, and patterns of repetition chosen by its creator. It is not surprising that many of the major methodological approaches to folklore begin with actual narratives.

ETHNOGRAPHIES AND COLLECTIONS OF LORE

A place to begin for the would-be folklorist of biblical narrative is with collections of folklore themselves. That Gunkel was able to appreciate and recognize "the folkloristic" in the Hebrew Scriptures is due, in part, to his familiarity with traditional stories prepared by modern European collectors. Collections such as those of the Grimms of Germany and Asbjørnsen and Moe of Norway are in many ways the sort of retold tales that are found in the Hebrew Bible. Much work has been done with the tales collected and preserved by the Grimms (Rölleke; Ellis; Bottigheimer; Zipes, 1988), showing how the tales were sometimes collected from middle class, literate women (Zipes, 1988:114), not from the oral-traditionally steeped, rural tellers projected by the Grimms's concept of "the folk" (Ellis, 1983:8,13,25–27), altered by the Grimms to tone down strong female characterizations (Zipes, 1988:74,114,124) and to eliminate bawdy references. They were also enhanced to accommodate the Grimms's own brand of German nationalism that sought in Zipes's view to "develop a genuine German heritage that would celebrate the democratic will and rights of the German people" (Zipes, 1988:113–14). The Grimms's versions tell us, in fact, about a particular Victorian culture and about the Grimms's own concerns and psychology (Zipes, 1988:28–61). On the other hand, the Grimms and their ilk provided fundamental source materials employed by early folklorists who approached questions of form and content and who then influenced subsequent scholarship. Tales such as those in the Grimm collections undergird some of Thompson's basic types and Propp's *Morphology* (see pp. 18–30). The case can be made that essential aspects of the stories remain visible under the Victorian veneer as relevant to all folk narration. Even as Victorian tales, they provide insight into the movement from oral to written literature and into the way humans tell stories in particular settings.

A similar resource is James George Frazer's *The Golden Bough*, a monumental multivolume collection of lore including tales, beliefs, customs, and rituals from all over the world and from a lengthy expanse of historical periods, catalogued according to Frazer's understanding of their central themes (e.g. Vols. I–II, Part 2 "The magic art and the evolution of kings"; Vol. IV, Part 3 "The dying God"; Vol. IX, Part 6 "The Scapegoat"). Frazer also prepared a special collection of "biblical lore," *Folklore in the Old Testament*, later expanded and revised by Theodor Gaster. Frazer's work was motivated by a particular interest in tracing the history of civilization and the origin of certain institutions such as sacred kingship and of certain motifs such as the great flood found in the biblical tale of Noah. Frazer speculates about the existence in "remote" times of "uniform zones of religion and society" in which certain customs and institutions existed, hints or remants of which are now found in various cultures (see for example *The Scapegoat*, Vol. 4, part 6:409). In a grander, less precise and more wildly ambitious way, his work anticipates that of the historic-geographic school of folklore (see below, pp. 15–18). Even while rejecting Frazer's assumptions and eschewing his particular concerns, one can employ *The Golden Bough* and Gaster's *Myth, Legend and Custom in the Old Testament* to become at home in the larger human realm of discourse to which aspects of biblical literature belong.

A similar grand resource is *Legends of the Jews*, Louis Ginzberg's retelling of the biblical narrative through the many voices of later Rabbinic midrashists who contemplated upon, elaborated upon, and reformulated biblical literature to convey messages and meanings relevant to their own times and concerns. Ginzberg's extensive footnotes direct the reader to primary sources with the incredible erudition of an earlier time. Some of these texts may preserve ancient variants of biblical narratives. They are fascinating indicators, in any event, of what can be done with the stuff of traditional narrative to create new narration.

While the work of the Grimms, Frazer, and Ginzberg have relevance to narration, Frazer's work to an even wider sweep of non-literary genres, works such as the new *Encyclopedia of World Proverbs* by Wolfgang Mieder are comparable resources for folk sayings. Like the biblical book of Proverbs, this collection takes sayings out of the context of human interaction and provides a new bookish context with its own agenda. Proverbs are indexed alphabetically by key words; under the key words are found comparable proverbs (in translation) from around the world. One should realize that a proverb's meaning is dependent on live context (Kirshenblatt-Gimblett, 1973) and that cultures vary in defining a "proverb" or in the way they do or do not classify sayings (Finnegan, 1970:390–93). Nevertheless, volumes such as Mieder's are valuable resources to acquaint oneself with the sorts of motifs and patterns of motifs found in a wide range of sayings from a broad range of cultures.

OLRIK'S "LAWS" OF SAGE AND THE AARNE-THOMPSON INDEX

Since Gunkel, the theories of Axel Olrik have been employed frequently by biblical scholars seeking to identify traits of traditional narration in the Hebrew Bible. In his "Epic Laws of Folk Narrative," Olrik outlined essential characteristics of a range of folklore including balladry, epic, folktale, and other narrative genres. His "laws" include the presence of no more than two characters to a scene, a linear single-strandedness of plot, repetitions in threes, a slow entrance and exit from the story. While Olrik's laws do appear to describe aspects of European folk traditions and to characterize many biblical narratives, their universality remains to be proven. Olrik, moreover, spoke of these laws "superorganically" without reference to artists or creators who partake of, continue, and innovate upon storytelling traditions. This is a serious omission in Olrik's theories, for they fail to treat context and composer. To suggest that a biblical narrative adheres to many of Olrik's laws does not tell all that much about a work's origin and genesis or about its meanings and messages. Olrik's laws certainly cannot be used to prove the antiquity of particular versions of biblical tales in relative chronologies (Van Seters, 1975:167–171; 183) or to prove their roots in oral, poetic tradition (Gunkel, 1966:40–58). Nevertheless students of the Bible should be aware of Olrik's work as a classic in descriptive folklore that has figured prominently in the work of biblical scholars.

Another classic work, available in its earliest form to Hermann Gunkel is the Aarne-Thompson Type Index, still an important tool for all students of folk narration. Antti Aarne sought to collect and classify the various folktales by the content of their essential storylines. This collection was greatly expanded by the American folklorist Stith Thompson. Each "type" of tale is assigned a number, and then the user is directed to various versions of that tale type found in a wide array of cultures. Thus "animal tales" are listed under numbers 1–299, "ordinary folktales," under numbers 300–1199, and so on. Cinderella, for example, is type 510A. Details change but the essential contours of these stories remain the same all over the world. Versions of Cinderella are found in China, Turkey, Poland, Italy, India, Indonesia, and many other countries and cultures. Thompson and his students also prepared a multivolume *Motif-Index of Folk-Literature,* seeking to catalogue the building blocks of the types: characters, settings, magic instruments, the smaller and reducible pieces of tradition that are combined to make up a tale. The motifs are catalogued by letter and number, and the *Motif-Index* directs the user to tales containing these motifs, but the motifs or elements of content described in the *Motif-Index* can be found also in nonnarrative folk genres such as proverbs, jokes, or riddles.

Aarne and Thompson collected and catalogued types and motifs in order to trace the genesis of tales geographically and historically—hence the designation of their school of scholarship as the historic-geographic school. Having much in common with the biblical scholar's tradition criticism and some forms of text criticism, these folklorists believe there was an earliest version of a tale, somewhere, sometime, that was shared, retold, and changed along the way. By studying the density of certain motifs in the tale as evidenced in specific geographic areas and periods of time and by tracking apparent changes in those motifs, members of the historic-geographic school prepare complex maps of a tale's path of development (see Thompson, 1965:414–74).

Thompson's method might be used to track the tradition history of some ancient Near Eastern tales, although the sample of available tales is probably too small. In any event, many scholars express doubts about the feasibility of the whole enterprise. Do not folktales always exist in multiple versions? Is there ever an earliest version? Are not some folktale types conceivably as old as storytelling itself? Cannot people from remarkably distant locations and cultures share certain proverbs or tale types because of the way humans are and because of the sorts of problems and pleasures their lives offer and not because of trade routes that somehow manage to link two distant lands? What is the role of creators in Thompson's scheme? (On the role of the creator/composer, see Finnegan, 1970:21,387.) The types seem to move and grow autonomously like a band of gypsy moths (Dundes, ed., 1965c:415; Abrahams, 1972a:26). Whatever one's views of Aarne and Thompson's rationales for collecting and classifying the tales, their taxonomic catalogues have become part of the language of the discipline of folklore studies. Scholars know what they mean when they discuss AT (Aarne-Thompson type no.) 510 or 922.

The type and motif indices allow scholars to compare biblical materials and a cross-cultural range of lore in order better to understand what is unique about the biblical telling but also significantly what is not unique. Niditch and Doran's study of stories of wise courtiers exhibiting the pattern of type 922, for example, becomes a point of departure for comparative cross-cultural and internal biblical analysis (see also Irvin's interesting work made possible by the Indices [1977; 1978]). Discovering that a battle account in the Bible is characteristic of many non-Israelite tales of war warns against drawing too many conclusions about Israelite military history from a biblical author's narrative war account. Before leaping to the conclusion that Abram's lying to Pharaoh in Genesis 12 is a dire ethical problem for the biblical writer, one does well to understand what this tale shares with the trickster tales of type 1542. The comparison shows that Gen 12:10–20 has to do not with the ethics of lying but with a marginal figure's use of disguise and marriage trickery to improve his status. The type indices teach much more about the worldview behind this story than one learns by superimposing a particular ethic or theology upon the tale.

Like adherence to Olrik's laws, the fact that many biblical tales can be "typed" according to Thompson's system seems to confirm that the Bible is rich in traditional lore (Dorson:19–20). Again, however, this allows for a broad definition of the traditional. Although more recent listings of tales in the indices often have been collected by modern folklorists using tape recorders and concerned with context and creators, many citations—even the titles of tale types to be found in the subject index to the Type Index (e.g. "Kaiser und Abt," "Cinderella")—come from old-fashioned, refashioned collections such as those of the Grimms, from classical Greek sources, and from the rich rabbinic tradition in which relations between oral and written literatures are indeed complex. The indices help to identify sorts of tales and lore in the spectrum of the traditional, but the spectrum is wide.

CAUTIONS IN PRACTICAL USE OF THE INDICES

The indices appear to be based on a sort of structuralism in which motifs build to form types. The structuralism, however, is of a very imprecise variety. Some types overlap in terms of the essential pattern of their content. An animal tale from types 1–299 may share an essential pattern about a trickster with a tale grouped among "ordinary folktales" (300–1199). These tales, catalogued apart from each other, are the same story except that the hero of one is an animal, the other a human. Content at a rather specific level sometimes disguises the underlying story patterns in the index and so one must search the index thoroughly when looking for biblical parallels. Similarly the same essential motif—for example "magic produces fertility"—may be found in many different categories in the *Motif Index* (see T510, T540, D1347, D1927). Finally, the line between the complex motif and the type is thin and some of the motif citations lead to good parallels for biblical narratives or the biblical narratives themselves (for example T481.4 "the Potiphar's wife plot"). Time is required to acquaint oneself with the indices and the way they work. They are the keys to a wealth of comparative materials and provide biblical tradition-historians an interesting parallel in the field of folklore to methodologies that seek to track traditions.

The weaknesses in Thompson's classifications and problems in using the indices stem largely from an ambiguity in defining content and structure and from the relative importance placed upon content rather than form in describing tales. Thompson's types are heavily weighted towards content. The other equally influential method in delineating folk narration is weighted towards form. The formalism of Vladimir Propp employs common denominator designations for elements of content and uncovers one essential shared pattern or structure in a set of Russian tales.

MORPHOLOGICAL-STRUCTURAL APPROACH

Although Propp's study is confined to numbers 50–151 of the Afanes'ev collection of Märchen or "wondertales," the specific morphology he uncovers and his overall morphological approach are very useful in approaching the components and combinations that make for forms of folk communication. In his famous *Morphology*, Propp's work is descriptive and does not deal with matters of creator, context, and meaning (contrast, however, Propp, 1984:11,50,110,115), but providing a convenient means of laying out the stuff of traditional literatures is, as Propp himself suggests, a first step in the thorough analysis of folklore.

Propp's steps in the action sequence of a narrative are the "functions" of the tale's characters: e.g. "hero *acquires* the use of a magical agent" (function XIV). This function may be specified in a variety of ways. The act of acquisition may involve a gift, a discovery, or a conquest, but the functions, however specified in any one tale, are "stable, constant elements of limited number" whose "sequence" is the same in every one of

18

Propp's sample of one hundred tales (Propp, 1960:21–22). The functions are the verbal part of a stable sequence. On the other hand, the "tale roles" or "dramatis personae" perform in or are acted upon by the functions. The villains, heroes, helpers and other actors thus move about in the sequence of functions, and each of these "roles" can be variously specified. The hero may be a third, none-too-promising son or an able prince. Thus Propp provides a model, a structure that can be colored or filled with content in various ways, but the underlying frame remains the same. His own work, of course, deals with narrative and with a limited set of a particular sort of narratives from a particular culture. For this reason, biblical scholars may run into trouble if attempting too woodenly to comprehend the traditional narratives of the Bible according to Propp's scheme. On the other hand, Propp provides an excellent methodological model as one searches for the Israelite tradition's own morphologies, whether they be in the narrative, wisdom, or prophetic traditions (See, for example, Jason's variations on Propp's scheme, applied to other types of tales and cultures [1971a, 1981, 1984]). Propp's work suggests a means of searching for underlying structural frames that make for the recurring literary forms of biblical literature. Culley's studies of action sequences in the Hebrew Bible (1976a; 1990) and Pamela Milne's study of Daniel (see her excellent bibliography [1988:293–309]) show how a great deal can be learned when Propp-influenced morphological approaches are cautiously and flexibly applied to the traditional narratives of the Bible (1988:177–262). Other interesting experiments with Proppian work and the Bible are Jack Sasson's study of the Book of Ruth and W. Soll's study of Tobit. Modern folklorists influenced by Propp's methodological approach include Heda Jason (1971a; 1981), Alan Dundes (1971; 1965a; 1965b); and Ben-Amos (1966). Their works provide excellent models for the folklorist of biblical literature.

The essentially morphological approach that explores the underlying grammar of pieces of folklore has been extended with success to other genres such as the riddle and the proverb (Dundes, 1971; Georges and Dundes). Dundes has suggested, in fact, that morphological structures are the keys to defining folk genres, which he views as universal folk forms, "filled" out or specified by creators within their own times, contexts, and cultures (on the structure of proverbs, see Dundes, 1975 in Dundes and Mieder; on riddles, see Georges and Dundes, 1963; see also Ben-Amos, 1976b:xxvii). If the historic-geographic method has something in common with the type of critical inquiry Bible scholars call

19

tradition history, then the structuralist-morphological approach has much in common with form criticism and indeed might guide the biblical scholar to become a better form critic.

PARRY-LORD-BYNUM-FOLEY

Each of the approaches discussed thus far has to do with the surface aspect of folk narrative and other folk genres, seeking ways to understand a story or a proverb in terms of a progression—motif to motif, function to function, or meaning unit to meaning unit. Another approach helpful in exploring this surface aspect of folklore is that of the students of early and oral literatures mentioned above. Lord and others who study the forms, composition, and transmission of early and oral literatures have made descriptive and classificatory contributions important to the study of folklore and the Bible. They begin at the level of words used to convey images and meanings, building to the analysis of the "motifs" or images they create, and finally explore the larger "themes" created by combinations of motifs. Their analyses of oral style provide methodological guidelines for the biblical scholar's examination of Israelite prosodic and prose styles. To acquaint oneself with Lord's work and that of his students and critics, excellent starting places are his classic and readable *Singer of Tales* and the various offerings in the ten-year-old journal *Oral Tradition* (See also works mentioned above in the discussion of "oral and written"). Understanding the relationship between formulas, motifs, and themes like an awareness of Thompson's outlines of types and motifs and Propp's sequence of functions, enhances the biblical scholar's analysis of literary forms and their relation to life settings in the methodology called form criticism. Lord's approach, in particular, encourages special attention to the texture of the text itself, the very words and phrases chosen by authors.

THE CHALLENGE IN DESCRIBING

Each of these ways of dealing implicitly or explicitly with the form and content of pieces of folklore leaves something unfinished. Olrik's sweeping laws, for example, do not distinguish between poetic and prose forms, and pay little attention to the specific details of "plot." Thompson is attuned to content and plot, but his content-based distinctions between tale types often obscure clear parallels in story structure between tales of different types. Propp's plot-based morphologies ignore specifics of content that are, in fact, central to understanding the special meanings and messages of any one version of a tale. Nor does his morphology suit all of Thompson's "types."

Lord and Bynum's "themes" and "motifs" allow for various convention-alized narrative structures as do Thompson's types and also for consider-able flexibility in defining and describing each theme and motif. Like morphologies, Lord's themes and motifs are shown to be filled out by creators in various ways. While Propp shows how various tales of specific content really share a common set of functions more generally described, Bynum is interested in the way the general is rendered specific. The "ge-neric" motif of "the underdog" can be specified in various "nominal" forms such as unemployed soldier, little tailor, or third son (Bynum, 1978:77–81).

THE "OVERLAY MAP" TECHNIQUE

Influenced by Lord and Bynum, my own teachers; by Thompson and Propp; and by Dundes and Ben-Amos's simplifications of Propp's lengthy sequence, I have suggested an overlay map approach to narrative struc-ture that allows for several levels of specificity in content (Niditch, 1987:23–69): At the generic level, virtually all narrative deals with a prob-lem and its resolution (or perhaps lack of resolution). Propp's opening function "lack" and his concluding "liquidation of lack" are attuned to this very basic aspect of story. As one turns over a leaf of the overlay map, one begins to see the contours of narration made more specific, a level I call, (after Propp, Dundes, and Ben-Amos) "the morphological." In the mor-phology of the underdog tales the problem is a "hero or heroine's lack of status," its resolution an "improvement in status." Motifs between lack of status and improvement are similarly more specific at this level. At a still more specific level called "the typological" (after Thompson), one paints the pattern with more detail, but the options for filling in the motif steps are numerous. The problem specified as marginality may be a condition of infertility or one of economic deprivation or political exile; the counter-parts of improvement in status would then involve having children or ac-quiring riches or reassertion of power. At this point, characterizations of heroes and villains become more important as do the relationships be-tween them. At this level one more or less tells the story; for example, a barren woman receives assistance from a deity that enables her to give birth to a son. This is a favorite story in the Hebrew Scriptures, a biblical type that is repeated over and over and yet it is rendered even more specific, at the individual level; for example, Rebecca is barren, Isaac prays to God, and God responds by granting the couple a birth of twins.

The "overlay map" technique uncovers some of the various ways one can describe the building blocks of narration and begins to concentrate on the ways in which the lore of the Bible is and is not unique. Context and content are multileveled. We seek better to understand the messages of individual Israelite writers, their particular contexts and problems, the recurring themes of the larger biblical tradition and the complex Israelite culture and history it reflects, a wider ancient Near Eastern context, and broader still the narrative patterns shared by human beings across cultures and times. One could certainly provide more "layers" to the map— a specifying of content, for example, between typological and individual layers—or fewer, as I do in a simplified application of my methodology in a study of the Samson narratives (Niditch, 1990), but the overlay map technique provides a means of understanding the surface levels of narrative content and structure. Such a method of entering into other folk genres such as jokes or proverbs could also be useful.

"DEEP STRUCTURE"

The name most associated with a deep-level or "paradigmatic" approach to narrative structure is Claude Lévi-Strauss. Lévi-Strauss' structuralism suggests that in addition to the relationships between sequential motifs in plots there exist deep, synchronic relationships between the components of narrative that have their own logic and wholeness apart from a tale's apparent story line. In Lévi-Strauss' view, these relationships have to do with people's innate tendency to see the world in pairs of contradictions: life versus death; nature versus culture; light versus dark; divine versus human. Beneath the surface of the self- and culture-revealing, value-rich traditional tales he calls myth, are embedded patterns or bundles of these dichotomies. The structuralist attuned to these underlying patterns is able to unravel the deepest meanings and concerns of the narratives. Such tales not only state contradictions—we humans long to be eternal but are ephemeral; we fear incest but suspect that our earliest ancestors were related in the forbidden way—but also reveal attempts to resolve, or better, to balance them. That is, the contradiction in question is never fully resolved. Through a dialectic of contradiction and mediation by narrative components that share characteristics of each side of the dichotomy, an unbearable disharmony is turned into a bearable balancing act. Tricksters, for example, are often key mediators in tales that deal with problems implicit in the origins and the ordering of the cosmos of which we, as humans, are a part, for they embody a host of contradictions within themselves. The serpent of Genesis 3 is such a trickster—wise yet foolish, eternal yet limited, human-like and animal-like.

Lévi-Strauss' paradigmatic studies lead to the underlying unity among various versions of a story—Freud's Oedipus and Sophocles's are, on a meta-cultural level, the same myth. The same deep structure can be found in them revealing some of our most basic concerns as humans. Lévi-Strauss' methodology taken to its logical end would seem to justify Joseph Campbell's sort of cross-cultural work in which ultimately all myths are one.

At the same time, Lévi-Strauss, the ethnographer, more often collects material from one group and finds in its myths the deep structural patterns of a particular culture. Both approaches are valid. As in much of folklore studies, pieces of lore may be studied in their humanly shared, virtually universal guises even while recognizing them as the expressions of individual creators who belong to particular cultural settings and moments in time.

Lévi-Strauss' work is well known in biblical studies (Oden; Polzin, 1977; Patte, 1960). The unfamiliar reader is directed to Lévi-Strauss' monographs and to the folklorist Bengt Holbek's recent study and critique (1987:340–45). Lévi-Strauss' work evokes many criticisms: Do all humans see the world in pairs? Are all variants of a narrative versions of the same myth? Where are the storytellers in Lévi-Strauss' scheme? Are they unconscious transmitters of culture and mirrors of human psychology somehow compelled to produce deep narrative structures that have to do with incest or the fear of death, even while they think they are telling a good story that has to do with other matters?

In any event, deep structuralist approaches can provide fresh insight into the symbolic underside of folk narration and into its dramatic counterpart in ritual. Deep structuralist approaches also have been applied in productive ways to other folk genres such as riddles (Scott). Holbek (1987:345–89) moreover, directs the reader to studies such as those of Elli Köngäs Maranda, Pierre Maranda, and Algirdas Julien Greimas that seek to combine Proppian and Lévi-Straussian models.

CONTEXT, MEANING AND MESSAGE: SELF, CULTURE, AND HUMANITY

The field of folklore is interdisciplinary. The first half of this chapter implicitly asks what the field of folklore draws from and what special contributions it makes to various types of literary study: genre studies, formalism, structuralism, studies in oral and early literatures, etc. The second half of this introduction to the field of folklore ranges even more broadly to the disciplines of history, sociology, psychology, anthropology, and women's studies. Each of these disciplines (or interdisciplines) has its own relationship to biblical studies as other volumes in the *GBS* Old Testment Series and an ample bibliography illustrate. In brief, we ask what special approaches to the contexts, meanings, and messages of biblical texts might be suggested by the ways in which aspects of these fields are mediated through the interdiscipline of folklore.

FOLKLORE, THE BIBLE, AND "HISTORY"

When dealing with meaning and context surely one important question is, do biblical narratives tell us about Israel's origins and history? Some might suggest that biblical scholars have been preoccupied with the reconstruction of history—history in a nineteenth-century, positivistic sense. If so much of Scripture looks like folklore in the ways described and defined above, then it is well to ask what folklorists have to say about history and its relationship to what they study.

Biblical scholars have already taken stock of Jan Vansina's study (1965) of "oral history" (for example Van Seters, 1975:153,158) His interest in the ways in which oral accounts may be used for historical reconstruction seems less relevant to a study of Scripture if we allow, as we did at the opening, for a broad definition of folklore that looks at the "traditionality" of style, structure, and content rather than at demonstrable orality. The question whether or not folk tradition preserves historical fact is still of interest to those who collect actual oral traditions (for example David M. Pendergast). Even more helpful for our purposes is Richard Bauman's observations in a study of "Performance and Honor in 13th Century Iceland." While he shows how some scholars have used traditional style material to reconstruct the past—much as biblical scholars have made suggestions about a premonarchic "patriarchal age" based on accounts from the period of the monarchy or later—his own methodological preference is to see how tellings reflect the period in which they are told. (Bauman, 1986b:134; so too Vansina, 1985:31–32) This emphasis stems in part from Bauman's interest in the performance event and in what Ben-Amos (1972) calls context. Without such a context some genres such as proverbs become quite ambiguous, caught between the times and settings that help to create meanings. Context also has to do with respect for creators of pieces of folklore, people who are set in culture, time, and place, with attention to their own voices, styles, and skills (see Hymes, 1981; 1985), although in Scripture the voices are often anonymous. Concern with the historical setting of the created composition rather than with historicity leads to biblical scholarship that is, in fact, very interested in "history." Such an approach treats biblical literature as coming from real people who had tastes, aesthetics, and talents, and who lived in settings—economic, political, ecological, cultural, and religious—that helped to shape who they were. It encourages us to search for these real people and their worlds rather than to check the accuracy of their information, interesting though their past (and ours) may be. It is, however, also an approach that refuses to explore the text solely in terms of its meaning to readers or that suggests that the text can be interpreted without attention to its author's intentions, conscious or subconscious. It is, then, an approach that steers a course between biblical scholarship as a means of historical reconstruction and biblical scholarship as a wholly reader-responsed variety of literary criticism.

FOLK ARTIST, AUDIENCE, AND SOCIOLOGY: QUESTIONS OF COMMUNITY AND CONTEXT

The sociological bent implicit in modern folklore involves the continuing effort to understand lore in the context of the folk. The types of questions folklorists pose concern matters of *Sitz im Leben* so important to form critics in biblical studies, although the latter do not always engage in genuine questions about creators of the material, its audience, and its social context. Form critics conclude more often than not that the life setting for many biblical compositions is "the cult," rather impersonally conceived. Folklorists ask questions about the economic status of composers and audiences, about their gender, their age, and their place in the community and search out the ways in which these factors are reflected in folklore. They ask about ways in which a proverb or joke or narrative in turn creates and affects a social dynamic to resolve tensions, to assert dominance, to reinforce or restructure certain patterns of relationship in families or communities (Kirshenblatt-Gimblett, 1974; Abrahams, 1972a).

Folklorists working with contemporary lore can assess the folk group by asking appropriate questions of its members and by observing them in person. Scholars who work with ancient traditions have no such luxury, but it might serve them well to pose such questions hypothetically. To whom might a tale such as Jacob's stealing of the blessing in Genesis 27 have appealed? What are attitudes to authority implicit in the tales of Joseph? Does the voice of the narrator leave telltale signs concerning gender in Judges 5? How might a riddle, now employed in a particular biblical narrative such as the Samson narrative, have functioned if posed by a real groom to his affines? What happens to the riddle in its current context? How many social shadings are available to a simple proverb "like mother/like daughter," depending upon the social setting? How does the prophet Ezekiel contextualize this flexible piece of lore to have it suit his message? These questions explore the various settings shaped by folk compositions and reflected in them and point to the transformations in meaning effected by a change in context.

THE SELF AND CULTURE: ANTHROPOLOGICAL APPROACHES

Biblical scholars already have available to them resources in anthropology and the Hebrew Bible (Culley and Overholt; Overholt; Wilson). Mary Douglas's study of the dietary laws in Leviticus that explores Israelite concepts of and symbolizations of "clean" and "unclean," "order" and "disorder" is well known as is Edmond Leach's structuralist study of "Genesis as Myth." R. R. Wilson, Robert Culley, Thomas Overholt, Burke Long, and others employ contemporary ethnographic data collected and analyzed by modern anthropologists to help shed light upon law, ritual, social institutions, and other aspects of Israelite culture that may be reflected in the literature of the Bible.

The anthropology of folklorists, like that of anthropologists who would not call themselves folklorists, involves the effort to understand cultures: the symbol systems through which they are expressed, formed, and maintained; the threads of relations defining families and larger social groups; the ways in which a particular cultural group at some point in its history responds to underlying "big" questions posed by all people, concerning the meaning of life, the inevitability of death, and the reasons for suffering. What is special about folklorists interested in or trained in anthropology is the emphasis they place on modes of expression—on "lore." How do the textures of tale-tellers' language and the folk media in which symbols express central concerns reflect and shape those very symbols and concerns? Dell Hymes's "sociolinguistic" approach blends fields of anthropology, folklore, and linguistics to interpret culture through its literary folk creations. In a similar vein, anthropologist John Middleton explores the ways in which modes of prophetic speech reflect the place of their speakers in a spectrum of social roles, from those most closely connected with the political and religious establishment to those peripheral to and outside the center of power. These links between medium, message, messengers, and social structure again point to central folkloristic concerns with texture, text, and context (see Ben-Amos, 1972) and can be extremely useful in exploring the literary forms of the Hebrew Bible and changes in those forms over time. The goal is to understand the composers, participants in lengthy literary traditions, and the ways they infuse ancient traditions with their own individual artistry, adapting them to their own times and to the concerns of their audiences. Why, for example, is an ornate and elaborate form of the symbolic vision found in Daniel and intertestamental works, whereas the form still recognizable in its morphology or common-denominator pattern of content is found in a much simpler version in Amos and Jeremiah?

THE INNER SELF REVEALED IN LORE: THE INDIVIDUAL AND HUMANITY— THE MOST PARTICULAR AND MOST UNIVERSAL

Psychologically oriented methodologies in folklore have been reviewed and discussed recently with clarity and insight by Holbek (1987:259–322 and bibliography; see also Dundes, 1988). The two forefathers of the western psychoanalytic tradition, Freud and Jung, were themselves interested in folk genres such as myth (Freud, 1913; Jung) and jokes (Freud, 1905) and in the symbolic stuff that lies behind them. In a sense, they themselves have shaped certain myths such as the Oedipus pattern in ways that have become a part of our own ways of looking at ourselves and others.

Holbek portrays Freud's approach to traditional narrative as rather down-to-earth and pragmatic, having to do with human experiences and emotions since birth, perhaps forgotten later in life but incorporated into the subconscious and affecting and shaping people's personalities. Traditional patterns of motifs, whether found in dreams or in waking stories, symbolically represent aspects of our development and maturation as people. Critical in this process of human development are relations with those in one's immediate family, the most basic aspect of and gauge of human development being sexual. The narrative dream is an effort to work through problems symbolically or a map indicating what the problems might be. The dreamer may project symbolically his sexual desire for mother onto someone else or repress it. Even the storyteller who, unlike the dreamer, selects his or her motifs and combines them consciously, reveals some of his or her hidden inner self, shared human concerns, and psychological puzzles in the basic typological patterns of his or

27

her stories. One should neither trivialize Freud with a pop version of his theories nor ignore their implicit sexism and Victorian roots. Like versions of pieces of folklore, Freud's approach to folklore has to do with the particular mind-set of its creator (his own personality and psychology) and the social-historical reality in which he worked. Nevertheless, Freud's emphasis on the process of self-definition, the ways in which persons are formed by childhood bonds and experiences in relation to and rebellion against their parents and siblings, and his emphasis on the conflict between *eros* and *thanatos* within each individual suggest ways of entering the most common stories and constellations of symbols human minds conjure. The Hebrew Scriptures on covert and overt levels are rich in these manifestations of character-forming inner conflict and conflict with close relatives, as Freud's student, Otto Rank, shows in his study of the pattern of the hero, a work that includes studies of tales of Joseph and Moses, and as Dundes controversially suggests in his study of Jesus (1980).

Freudian folklorists can be accused of seeing menstruation behind every little redcap (Red Riding Hood; Fromm, 1951:240–41) or a womb under every reference to an oven (see, for example, the Freudian work of Róheim). As Holbek has shown, the Freudian interpretation of narratives often depends upon the psychology of the interpreter, such an interpretation being one of a wide array of "reader responses," as the interpreter shapes and reforms the piece of folklore (Holbek, 1987:318–19; see also Röhrich, 12). Nevertheless, like Lévi-Strauss, Freud leads us to look under the surface of stories, riddles, jokes, and other forms even while self-consciously questioning our own interpretations of them (as Fewell and Gunn implicitly do).

Holbek suggests that Freudian analysis of the symbols and patterns evidenced in folk narration and other genres looks toward the past; the analysis is grounded in the clinical concern with troubled patients' experiences before analysis. It is a pragmatic approach seeking to unlock the past to explain the patient's current malady and release him or her from it—a means of socializing the patient to enable him or her to "fit in." (1987:259–92) Jungian analysis, according to Holbek, looks to the future and is more spiritually and individually oriented in its concern to help the patient reach a best self, one who is not only at peace with himself or herself but who experiences the fulfillment of self-consciousness. (292–314)

The symbols and patterns relevant to folklore studies for Freud had to do with human beings' coping mechanisms such as repression or projection. Symbols fall into identifiable and interpretable categories because all humans do share the repertoire. Jung developed this notion of shared repertoire more mystically and spiritually with his concept of archetypes. Each human being's mind at birth is already infused with certain key and fundamental symbolic images: for example, the archetype of the Mother, or the archetype of the anima. Each of these archetypes has a negative and a positive aspect, and they are all involved in a drama or spiritual odyssey in which the vessel who contains them, the human being, can reach enlightenment or consciousness by bringing the conscious self into awareness of the unconscious. The recurring narrative patterns and constellations of motifs that characterize works in the traditional mode are evidence of the archetypes and of the ways they take creative turns in pieces of human invention. Such traditional works reveal not only the concerns, problems, and states of being of the particular storytellers and artists, but also the shared set of symbols uniting all humans. Jung offers an explanation for why S. Thompson is able to define and find so many examples of his cross-cultural types and motifs.

Jung's work, like that of his student Erich Neuman, makes one think deeply about the archetypal significance of biblical narratives, characterizations, and images. For example, Jael (Judg 4:17–22; 5:24–27) might be viewed not only as an Israelite patriot or biblical heroine but also as a manifestation of the negative side of the archetypal feminine in a man's tale—alluring but dangerous, apparently nurturing but actually murderous. Like that of the female Anti-Wisdom of Proverbs, her sexuality leads to death.

WOMEN'S STUDIES AND FOLKLORE

As in so many disciplines, the interdiscipline of women's studies has provided new and valuable perspectives on folklore, both the field of study and the materials studied. Given that so much of the traditional material in Scripture deals with women—law, rituals, narratives, proverbs, and riddles concerning women—it is to be expected that approaches of folklore and women's studies will lead to important insights.

The interests of students of women's studies and folklore fall under various headings. First are questions about women creators of folklore, their social contexts and possibly gender-based worldviews. Are women of a particular folk group more likely to tell stories of certain genres rather than others and why (Mills; Jason, 1984)? Is there such a thing as a women's voice? How does a person's gender in a particular social setting affect the way he or she tells a tale, the motifs chosen, the images drawn within a conventionalized type (Holbek, 1987:576–77; Baldwin; Mitchell; Yocum)? For those who work with ancient literatures, always unsure of authors' identities and genders, the problem might at first seem a bit like Daniel's challenge to tell the dream and its interpretation. It is, however, possible to speculate upon Deutero-Isaiah's birthing imagery employed within stylized traditional literary forms (Isa 42:14b; 49:15) or to notice that so many of the tricksters in the Hebrew Bible are women—marginal people who make their way behind the scenes through wily deception and trickery (Gen 27; 31:19,33–35; 38). The contexts of these tricksters usually has to do with the private rather than the public realm, their power home based and related to the successes of their male children. Could the author of Deutero-Isaiah be a woman? Could stories of Rebecca, Rachel, and other biblical women have been composed by female storytellers? Could there have been professional "wise women" in ancient Israel—mediators working through dramatic improvisation, folk actresses (see Camp, 1990)? Are there a host of other female folk artists—weavers of proverbs, singers, priestesses, prophets all practicing forms of improvisation upon culturally shared patterns, women to whom the edited Scripture alludes only in hints?

A second group of questions concerns the way women and men and their attitudes are portrayed in folklore. Such questions have to do with the way dominant cultural attitudes toward women may be imbedded in narratives or riddles that even a woman composer might produce and involve finding cultural keys in folklore concerning the status of women. Also involved are interests in psychoanalytical questions about men's and women's attitudes toward sexuality, spouses and parents, children or aging. Fields of sociology and psychology thus intertwine with women's studies and folklore. Does a piece of folk art or literature reveal men's fear of women, or vice versa? Such questions about gender-based attitudes implicit in lore seem especially appropriate in studying the figure of Anti-Wisdom who lures young men to Sheol (Prov 5:1–6; 7:5–27). Even a woman may employ proverbs or weave stories that are overtly sexist if she has integrated within herself the dominant culture. Her tales, as much as those of male tellers, may eloquently testify to the androcentrism of a culture and to the roles regularly played by and expected of men and women. Women, moreover, may take on a status as symbol in one or another folk text or art work revealing deeply held human emotions about relationships, for example, between children and mothers or more culturally bound information about a group's attitudes to relations among kin.

Much of the traditional material studied by folklorists is not lore in process but, like the Hebrew Bible, material that has been edited and reformulated. The reformulators are themselves creators, artists, and composers—participants in the tradition and the traditional. Their own attitudes have become a part of the traditional literature we study much as the Brothers Grimm are now part of the German folk tradition, having for better or worse reshaped the stories they collected in significant ways that reflect their psychology, tastes, sense of propriety, and so on. Scholars of European folklore, themselves redaction critics who have gone back to the Grimms' original notes and early prepublished manuscripts, have noted in particular how the Grimms toned down pictures of strong capable women that came from some of their female informants (see Ellis:37–71). The passive Cinderellas and Snow Whites in turn have become a powerful force as role models for young girls who hear them (see Zipes, 1983a; 1986:231; Bottigheimer, 1987:160; Rowe:209–26). Has a similar process affected the biblical tradition? The tale of Miriam in Numbers 12 richly implies such a process at work. And yet the strength of other wise and wily women shines through. Indeed contrary to what the later Christian and Jewish exegetical tradition has led us to believe, Eve is one of them.

2
Folklore and Biblical Narrative: A Study of Genesis 3

SOUNDINGS: SOURCES, SIN, AND ANCIENT NEAR EASTERN PARALLELS

The story about Adam, Eve, the tree, and the serpent has generated an enormous bibliography over the years (see, for example, Westermann's masterful review). Treatments of Genesis 3 serve as an excellent barometer for the state of our discipline while reflecting a larger Western cultural tradition shaped, in part, by understandings of Eve's story.

It is not the goal of this study to take issue with the many and varying analyses of Genesis 3. Rather, by taking soundings in three of the most influential commentaries of the last forty years we are able to explore the contours of the discussion among modern, mainstream biblical scholars and then to make an alternate, biblical folklorist's proposal for study. How might the approach influenced by folklore studies lead to differing emphases and fresh nuances in interpretation—to an appreciation of aspects of Genesis 3 not always drawn out by more typical works of biblical scholarship?

The commentaries that provide the foil are Gerhard von Rad's 1956 study (English ed., 1961); E. A. Speiser's Anchor Bible commentary (1964); and Westermann's *Genesis*, vol. 1 (1974; English ed., 1984). Each scholar, of course, has his own interests and bents. One would expect von Rad's theological interests to be especially strong and so they are; Speiser's interest in ancient Near Eastern backgrounds is marked; and Westermann, while covering these areas, is also attuned to the sorts of patterns and parallels in content and structure that concern students of folklore.

Remarkably, however, even allowing for the uniqueness of each scholar's approach, their analyses share the same framework. All three treat the narrative in the context of the theological interests of the Yahwist source (von Rad:95; Speiser:25; Westermann:192; 196; 65–66). Speiser writes humanistically of the "spiritual experience of a whole nation"; von Rad more normatively and melodramatically of "sin and shame" as "the stigmata of the Fall in man" (88) and of "an earth under the domination of misery" (92); and Westermann sounds Dostoyevskian in describing a tale of "crime and punishment," suggesting further that in "J" the Fall is balanced by the covenant with Abraham (193, 196). For Westermann, the central question of Genesis 3 is "Why is a person who is created by God limited by death, suffering, toil, and sin?" (277)

All three scholars, moreover, endeavor to take Yahweh off the hook, as it were, for so jealously guarding his divine prerogatives. For von Rad, the serpent in Gen 3:5 uses the "ancient and widespread idea of God's envy to cast suspicion on God's good command" (86; see also Westermann:273). Speiser suggests that the serpent's words in v. 5 (confirmed by Yahweh's own words in v.22) merely mean that the author is employing "a literal application of a motif that Hebrew tradition took over from Mesopotamia centuries earlier." Thus "God's envy" does not betray aspects of a deep-seated, genuine Israelite worldview. Westermann suggests that God intends with his warning not to eat of the tree "to bring knowledge and death together in a way that is very mysterious" (240). Thus, perplexing though the prohibition is, it is somehow part of God's plan.

Though von Rad is weakest in this regard (95), all three scholars draw comparisons with appropriate ancient Near Eastern materials, especially tales of lost immortality in the Gilgamesh Epic (Speiser:26–28; Westermann:246–47). The ancient Near Eastern comparisons drawn by Speiser and Westermann tend to involve either individual motifs at a quite specific level (the forbidden fruit) or brief associations between such motifs (for example, the link between a snake and the loss of immortality) and not the whole story. Even while suggesting, like Speiser, that Genesis 2–3 "had a pre-history both in Israel and in the Ancient Near East," Westermann emphasizes that the overall pattern of the story of Genesis 3 shares more with "primitive" tales of world creation from Africa and elsewhere than with any of the cosmogonies of "the great classical traditions" (54–55). I understand Westermann's argument as follows: The roots of Genesis 3 are in Israel's primitive past, deep in a lengthy tradition-history that includes prewritten stages, rather than in the Bible's contemporary world that includes contact with the great civilizations of the ancient Near East (55). Westermann thus engages in his own idiosyncratic historical-geographic exercise, based on very little evidence and on rather outmoded contrasts between primitive and advanced cultures. Even if his conclusions are suspect, he, like Gunkel, does begin to work in terms of story patterns found within Genesis 1–11 and does attempt cross-cultural comparison. Ultimately, however, he, like Speiser and von Rad, approaches the tale with a sober and righteous seriousness, grounded in Jewish and Christian concepts of sin. All three scholars fail to do justice to the tale's tone, its characterizations, or its plot. If we are to approach Genesis 3 as folklorists, we must ask how we would interpret the narrative if we did not hold it to be a foundation myth, sacred Scripture in our own religious traditions.

The folklorist begins not with assumptions about the tale's place in some source's grand plan, nor with searches for this or that element of content in non-Israelite ancient Near Eastern tales, but with the story—its underlying pattern of content.

AN OVERLAY MAP FOR GENESIS 3

All narrative begins with a situation. In order for a story to develop, events must intervene to affect the situation and either restore the status quo or create a new situation. This essential generic narrative pattern lies behind all stories. When the disruption involves the breaking of an implicit or explicit prohibition, a range of narrative options opens up: A hero may be told never to look behind a certain door, does so, and sees an image of the most beautiful girl in the world. He must set out to find her and the story moves on to adventures in his quest. The status quo has been altered. A hero may take a rose that does not belong to him (Grimms's version of *Beauty and the Beast*) or steal some rapunzel plants from a witch's garden (Grimms's *Rapunzel*) and thereby place at risk a heroine whose problems become central in the story.

In Genesis 3 and in a cross-cultural range of cosmogonic world-ordering tales, the status quo is specified as an ideal situation, for example, a world without work and of peaceful coexistence among living beings. The specification of the motifs, of course, depends upon the culture and authors—their notions of what constitutes "ideal." The outcome of the broken prohibition is a state more like reality. Again the specific symbolizations or cameos of reality are important keys to the world of the tale's author and audience. The morphology tracing a pattern from ideal to reality is the one outlined by Westermann who cites tales from Africa. The pieces of the pattern all appear in various forms in Thompson's *Motif-Index* (Golden Age A1101.1, Tabu Broken C40, End of Golden Age

C939.4) leading us to an even wider range of tales exhibiting this world-ordering morphology. Works such as those of Frazer (1911–15) and Gaster (1981) also lead to a host of stories sharing this morphology. Many of these narratives, as Gaster notes (1:32), were no doubt influenced by Genesis 3, as missionaries spread the biblical tales among indigenous non-European populations. Many of the versions are in collections rewritten by unscientific collectors from field notes or memory, but others such as the interesting few South American examples excerpted below have been collected with attention to the gender and age of the informants and other criteria important to modern folklorists. The pattern is now found world-wide in a variety of settings and cultures, and the important point for the interpreter is that the morphological pattern of Genesis 3, even if not indigenous to African or native American groups, is retold and shaped in native stories that have become relevant within their own cultures because of certain very basic, existential concerns shared by all human beings. The presence of this morphology worldwide does have relevance for the way we read Genesis 3—not to explain that it is an example of Israelite primitive literature, whatever that means (see Westermann above p. 34), but to remind us of certain underlying themes that are found in all versions of the morphology, no matter how they are specified at the typological and individual Israelite levels: (1) Reality is irreversible. (2) Nevertheless, an image of life better than reality is preserved in the narrative. We all need such imaginings—they encapsulate ideals and hope. And yet (3) reality is made more acceptable because paradoxically humans are somehow responsible and not responsibile for their lot in life. These formative events happened before our time so long ago. How can we be blamed? Nevertheless, reality came about because of what our own ancestor heroes and heroines did. A comforting ambivalence is thereby established that implies we deserve our troubles and yet are personally not responsible for them. A certain capriciousness characterizes the conditions we live in. We might as well accept the uncontrollable serendipity in life.

A lengthy tale of early times was collected by Anthony Seeger from a Gê woman of Brazil named Mbéni. She was approximately fifty years old and told the story in her house with her daughters and grandchildren listening. In one episode the narrator explains:

> The rains come and wet the soil. They live in the
> village for several months. Then the woman's husband
> goes hunting and says: "I am going hunting, and I am
> going to look at the garden." The woman says: "Go

ahead." He goes to look for the garden, and arrives there. Well, the corn silk is yellow, the manioc is in the ground, the *mbrai* is on the vine, the *kara* is in the ground, the *waiyari-so* is in the ground. Gourds, beans, small beans, there are many crops. Going from side to side the brother-in-law looks at the garden and goes home. They stay in the village for a while longer, and he returns to look at the garden. Now the corn stretches out across the garden, and is still white; it still has few kernels. He goes home. The woman asks him: "How is it?" He replies: "Let's go, your mother has given us crops but they are not ready yet." "All right." Later he returns to the garden, goes to look at it, and it is ready. The men go to the garden and break off all the corn and take a lot. As soon as they break it off, more corn grows back. As soon as they dig up the manioc, more grows back.

A lazy man says: "Let's go pick some corn. Let's get some corn." "All right." They go to the corn in the garden and are breaking it, when suddenly one of the leaves cuts the man's hand. "Ouch, ouch, ouch!" he shouts. "This bad corn cut my hand. Let it all be finished, let it be finished. Let the garden be empty." He is angry at the corn. "Oh, your mother will be sad and go back to the river where the mouse lived," the people tell each other. When they arrive they speak to each other. The woman says: "We have our new (seed) corn, we have our new corn. Your mother-in-law told me that it won't grow any more." So now the husband goes and cuts a new garden, and when the old garden is empty, they plant more. They plant corn, and manioc, and when they harvest it, it all dries. The owners of the maize pick it, and break it off, and the garden becomes empty.

We have lived like that ever since. When it is harvested, the garden is empty! That is why the gardens are empty. Your mothers, your grandmothers tell us why it empties. Now the people make gardens and plant maize and manioc, and that is the way it is. That is it.

Wilbert and Simoneau, 1984:153–54

An episode in another Gê tale of beginnings concerning the stealing of fire tells of "boy's" experience with "jaguar":

He met the jaguar and told him he had killed his wife.
"That does not matter," answered he. At home he gave
the boy a lot of roast meat in addition and told him to
follow along the creek, then he would be sure to reach
his tribe. But he was to be on guard: if a rock or the
aroeira tree called him, he should answer but he was to
keep still if he heard the gentle call of a rotten tree. In
two days he was to return and fetch the fire.

The boy moved along the brook. After a while he
heard the rock shout and answered. Then he heard the
call of the aroeira and again answered. Then a rotten
tree cried out, and the boy, forgetting the jaguar's warning, answered it too. That is why men are shortlived; if
he had answered only the first two, they would enjoy as
long life as the rocks and the aroeira trees.

Wilbert and Simoneau, 1978:174

Another tale from the Bororo of Brazil is as follows:

> In the old days certain spirits tended the corn plan-
> tations, and the Bororo were able to pick beautiful ears
> of corn, big and uniformly shaped. Burekóibo, father of
> all the spirits, himself planted a cornfield that grew
> splendidly.
>
> One day the women went to his plantation, and
> while breaking off the ears of corn one of them was hurt
> by a splinter from a stalk. Made careless by the pain,
> she exclaimed: "Burekóibo hurt my hand!" She should
> never have complained like that, for her rashness did
> all the Bororo lasting harm.
>
> Burekóibo, with the keen understanding so typical
> of the spirits, at once found out about her disrespect
> and pronounced his sentence: "I won't plant any more
> corn, and I will no longer prepare nutritious food for
> you. You yourselves will have to cultivate the fields.
> When you want to plant you'll have to clear the ground,
> cut down trees and bushes, and pull up weeds. Only in
> that way will you be able to make the plants grow well."
>
> When the Bororo, following these instructions, had
> their plantations ready and the corn was ripe, Bure-
> kóibo called his son Bópe Jóku Babičó and ordered him
> to go to the Indians and ask: "My grandfathers, my
> grandfathers, what are you doing?" He was to report

the answers to his father. When Bópe Jóku Babičó asked the question, some of the Bororo answered well, others spoke curtly, and some even insulted him. He returned at once to Burekóibo who, informed of the attitudes of the Bororo, said: "Those who answered curtly shall get long very thin ears of corn. Those who insulted you shall get small ears without grains. But the ones who answered well shall have large, handsome ears with good grains."

It is because of this punishment that today the ears of corn in the Bororo plantations are no longer all the same; some are large, others have hardly any husks, and some are very thin. Because of the uncertainty of their harvests, the Bororo usually request the protection of Burekóibo at planting time, with these words: "My grandfather Burekóibo, give us ears as big as *acuri* nut clusters." They make this plea because Burekóibo produced very large ears of corn when he was cultivating the fields of the Bororo.

Wilbert and Simoneau: 1983, 86–87

The morphology as found in Genesis 3 carries the same thematic weight: The ideal imagined offers an earlier life better than reality. The reality is not temporary but for all time and it corresponds to an author's conception of the real world. Like the boy adopted by the jaguar, Eve need not have transgressed the prohibition but such characters always do. Without the breaking of the prohibition there would be no story. And so, we sons of Adam and daughters of Eve suffer the deprivations of reality for some reason—there is an order to existence—and yet at the same time we can lay the blame upon ancestor heroes and heroines who are circumscribed by the contours of ancient narratives about the beginning. We may as well accept the consequences of their actions over which we have no control and make the best of it. These themes still dominate Genesis 3 and are quite different from "crime and punishment" and "the stigmata of sin." Westermann might reply that in its current form, Genesis 3 introduces interests that alter the basic morphology shared with the Brazilian tales. An Israelite author has molded its tone and characterizations to be about an all-powerful God with a divine plan, a sinful and disobedient humanity, reality as a punishment and a reminder of our shortcomings. A close look at the way Genesis 3 specifies the morphology tracing the passage from ideal to reality says much about its author's concerns, interests, and culture, but the basic thrust of the morphology as described above remains strong.

What is the ideal situation to the author of Genesis 2–3? How exactly is it lost? And what is the changed status like? As in the Brazilian tales, the early time is one of ease and plenty. The fear of famine and the imagining of no such fear lie behind this tale along with acknowledgement of the need for strenuous and often frustrating work among subsistence farmers, work that too often yields little. The problem of hunger is the "lack" with which so many traditional narratives begin (for example, Hansel and Gretel). Carol Meyers (95–121) finds a setting for the particular fears implicit in Genesis 3 in the pioneer highland economy that predates the monarchy. Whether or not we can set the date of the tale so precisely, it does seem to reflect such basic agrarian concerns and realities. Two first people, a man and a woman, are in a fertile garden, and are provided all its bounty except for the fruit of one forbidden tree.

In the imagined ideal, animals and humans coexist, for all are vegetarians. The author does not comment on whether or not the humans are mortal, but has God threaten death should they eat from the tree. They are "naked and not ashamed." (2:25). They do not acknowledge their sexuality and are unmarked by the clothing that connotes identity and confers status. As the scene with the snake indicates, they are incapable of discriminating between good and evil. As God's words following the breaking of the prohibition indicate, until then they have lacked clear work roles in life, lacked a pecking order between them.

The particular imagining of an ideal world found in an Israelite author's Genesis 3 suits the condition that the anthropologist Victor Turner has called "communitas" or community as distinguished from the condition of being in "society" (1967). Turner notes that "communitas" as symbolically represented typifies those who are making ritual rites of passage in traditional societies from childhood to adulthood, from virginity to marriage, and so on. The middle ground between the old status and the new, shared by the initiates or passengers, is characterized by absence of rank between them, no differentiation or hierarchy, lack of "property insignia or secular clothing indicating rank or role" (95–96). In such ritual passages people return, in a sense, to being "naked and not ashamed," briefly recapturing that early time before responsibility, structure, and a place in society.

God's words to Adam and Eve after they eat from the tree make clear the contrast between community, with its lack of emphasis on hierarchy, and society with its structure, work roles, and hierarchy. Now the woman is over the snake, the man over woman. His role is to till the ground with difficulty, hers is to work by him and bear children. Their lives are no longer static, but clearly include the rhythms of birth; maturation with responsibility, hardship, and pain; family roles such as child, wife, or husband; and of course at the end death—in short, reality.

And yet, having explored in somewhat more detail this Israelite version of the cosmogonic morphology we cannot conclude that it is about sin or mortality or "why a person who is created by God is limited by death, suffering, and sin" (Westermann, 1984:277). Sin is nowhere mentioned in Genesis 3, and death is only one feature of reality; nor does the author imply a contradiction between the Great Creator's work and what happens to his creation. The outcome is as expected as the recurring traditional narrative pattern that tells about it, made inevitable by the prohibition in 2:17.

The abiding underlying concern in Genesis 3 is the passage from absence of structure—and therefore lack of disharmony—to structure, reality, and differences that lead to enmity. One might be tempted to conclude that such an image of the ideal comes from a highly structured society, a state rather than a prestate society. Of course, every society, every culture is by definition characterized by an order of some kind. Nevertheless, the Israelite writer is especially articulate in his pining after a particular kind of harmony. This tale is not just about hunger or death but about an even wider range of questions concerning the mode of being human in the world.

In support for this sinless interpretation of Genesis 3 one notes that other Israelite contributors to the biblical tradition do not allude to Genesis 3 to describe the coming of sin and death in the world. Adam and Eve's story is never mentioned as a symbol of sin and death. The one questionable passage in Hos 6:7 (kĕādām) should be translated "at Adam," Adam being a place name (Josh 3:16) in parallelism with Gilead (Hos 6:8). The primeval events synonymous with sin in the larger tradition are those involving the destruction of Sodom and Gomorrah (as in Isa 1:10; Ezek 16:48–49). Ezekiel knows of an Eden tale quite different from Genesis 3 involving a rebellion of the gods theme comparable to those of the Book of Enoch and Isaiah 14. For Ezekiel, humans in Eden commit and discover iniquity, but his story is not Genesis 3 (Ezek 28:12–19). It is interesting that the vision of Paradise to which Israelites hope to return—their "myth of eternal return" in Eliade's words—includes boundless fertility, peace, and, in the Isaianic tradition, a softening of the boundaries that distinguish the living creatures on earth; wolves lie down with lambs, bears feed with cows, lions eat straw, and children play with

41

asps and adders (Isa 11:6–9). Certainly the capacity not to transgress—to be one with God and filled with his knowledge—is also part of many writers' concept of paradise; these are part of a larger vision of utopian harmony that is a basic human ideal. Fear of the consequences of transgressing authority and the recognition of higher authority are the flip side of the utopian vision, what society most means. It is also interesting to see how this theme is worked out in Genesis 2–3. To do so one must explore the way in which presociety becomes society, concentrating especially on the characters involved.

GOD

In spite of modern biblical scholarship's engagement with tradition-histories and firm belief in source criticism, it is quite surprising how much the God of Genesis 1 intrudes upon interpretations of Genesis 2–3. The events narrated in Genesis 2–3, it is suggested, have to be understood in terms of God's larger plan, however mysterious. Modern scholars try to make sense of what they consider to be an all-powerful, all-knowing deity who appears to fear humans' possible acquisition of knowledge and immortality, who has to deal with humans on the loose, who has tricky snakes sneaking around his back, and who must adjust in a totally ad hoc way to the events around him. Not unlike all the great heads of pantheons such as Odin or Zeus, he is a powerful creator god—more powerful than all other forces—but he can be tricked, becoming subject to the wiles of those whom he has created, such as Loki, Prometheus, the snake, Adam and Eve. He is, in short, a parent.

Freud, of course, makes much of God as the father to be feared—the children's authority, law-giver, enforcer, and protector, while Jung and Neumann write of the archetype of the mother—nurturing, loving, and supportive in its positive aspect, smothering, swallowing, capable of drowning and denying nourishment with its power over life. However, as all the great mythmakers have understood, there is, from the parents' perspective, an aspect of the parental role that involves total power-lessness. The Mesopotamian deities Tiamat and Apsu cannot stop the noise of the younger gods, while El, head of the Canaanite pantheon, faces and fears threats of bodily harm from his dear girl Anat. This is the sort of god the father encountered in Genesis 2–3, and like parents everywhere, he does the best he can. Having done his good work of creation, molding the man, attending to his companionship, and forming the man's counterpart from his rib, and having warned the man about the tree of knowledge (v. 17), God leaves. He reappears once the prohibition is broken, calling "Where are you?" The man's excuse for hiding only reveals his guilt in the matter of the tree. "Who told you, you were naked? Did you eat from the tree that I commanded you not to eat from?" (3:11) God curses the snake to reptilian status (3:14–15) and sets the humans' terms of reality: work, birthing with pain, and dying. God does not carry out his threat to kill the humans. He is thus not a consistent authoritarian—again the analogy with the parent seems apt. He clothes them with skins, still a caring provider, but now in a less than perfect world animals are killed for their use to humans. Finally, in v. 22 he reveals himself to be the deity the snake knows so well in v. 5. He speaks to his councilors: "The human has become like one of us knowing good and evil." He decides to cut his losses, banishing the man and the woman from the garden lest they eat also from the tree of life and join the ranks of the immortals. In short he has had no divine plan, operates on a short term, ad hoc basis, and sometimes his threats are not fully carried out. The world and all that is in it are his to control, for he is the most powerful of beings, but the snake trickster and God's human creations are able to shake the world and shape it this way and that, leaving the all-powerful one to react, reassert his authority, and move on from there.

EARTHY AND DIVINE: BROKEN BOUNDARIES

Nor have the man and woman lost closeness to God with the intense alienation described by von Rad and Westermann. They are no closer than they were before and he is no more distant. They are less close to becoming gods but this is as it must be, for another theme that accompanies the passage from harmony to reality is the dichotomy between the divine and the human, a certain law of territoriality that is breached not only in Genesis 3 but also in its narrative counterparts in 6:1–4 and 11:1–11.

In the Israelite versions of the cosmogonic morphology, the prohibition implicit in Gen 6:1–4 and 11:1–11 and explicit in Genesis 3 involves the mixing of the divine and human. In two of the Brazilian myths cited above, the broken implicit prohibition involves complaining about a divine creation (leaves of the corn plant). In the Israelite tradition preserved in Genesis 1–11, a boundary between the human realm and the divine is crossed three times, and this is what leads to a change in the status quo, the move to reality. In Genesis 3, the crossing involves eating God's food from God's tree and absorbing the divine power of discrimination; fruit, as so many artists in the tradition have noted, is a symbol closely associated with sexuality—the rich juicy stuff containing seeds. In Gen 6:1–4 the boundary crossing overtly involves sex—the sons of god, divine beings, taking wives from among the beautiful daughters of humankind. Then God places a limit on the human lifespan. This all-too-brief tale in four verses probably has longer, richer, now lost variants in the ancient tradition (cf. traditions preserved in the Book of Enoch). In Genesis 11, the boundary is spatial as humans who are described as speaking one language—what better symbolization of harmony between all humans—attempt to build a tower to God's realm in the sky and are halted, "punished" with the confusion of languages that separates person from person and establishes society and reality with its diverse makeup. The key pairs in Genesis 3, ideal and reality and divine and human, thus intertwine in a particular Israelite version of a widespread cosmogonic pattern.

Thus far the folklorist's approach had led to a host of traditional-style tales that share the morphological pattern of Genesis 3. This morphology in turn suggests certain underlying concerns shared by all humans who tell such stories and leads to exploring the psychology behind them. Turning to the special Israelite version found in Genesis 3, we find, with help from the ritual and symbol studies of the anthropologist Victor Turner, that the central theme of the story involves the contrast between life without strict structure and hierarchy and life with a clear hierarchy and statuses, a contrast between the ideal of community and the reality of society. Other representatives of Israelite tradition echo Eden not to write about sin but to evoke the time of harmony.

We have been led to an imagining of God as parent, all-powerful and authoritarian, but neither totally consistent nor totally obeyed. Finally, the Israelite version of the motif of broken prohibition emphasizes the distance between the divine and the human realms.

CULTURE BRINGERS: SNAKE, WOMAN, AND MAN

In many cultures a character called a trickster is involved in the process of world ordering. Such characters are found in a variety of folktale plots involving the challenge by a character of lesser status to the establishment or authority by means of deception. The trickster succeeds in changing his situation or that of those around him, but never completely gets away with his or her trickery. His success is of a shaky unstable variety. I have explored tales of tricksters in connection with Jacob, Rebecca, Rachel,

Laban, and other biblical characters (Niditch, 1987; 1990). When the challenge is to the great creator god and involves the time of beginnings before the coming of reality, the trickster is intimately involved in the cosmogonic world-ordering process.

Westermann brushes aside the suggestion that the snake is such a trickster. He notes that the snake is distinguished by the capacity to speak and by its "knowledge of divine secrets" and that "African narratives often speak of the clever animal in just this way." "An animal (that can also talk) has almost always a role to play in the narrative cycle of 'how death came into the world'" (Westermann, 1984:238). Yet, concludes Westermann, "One should not compare the function of a trickster of this sort with that of the serpent" (238). Why not? What Westermann has described is, in Lévi-Straussian terms, a mediator.

As discussed in chapter 1, Lévi-Strauss suggests that human beings symbolize some of their deepest concerns and ambivalences in contradicting or contrasting pairs of narrative motifs. The mediator is a motif halfway between the opposites, a narrative element that shares from each side of the contradiction. A morphological analysis of Genesis 2–3 has revealed two major contrasts around which the motifs of the story are patterned: (1) the passage from an ideal prestructure and "community" to the reality of hierarchy and "society," a passage that emphasizes and is effected by (2) the distinction between the divine and the human. The snake alone in the ideal time embodies and confuses the traits of the divine and human, for he thinks and discriminates; he is able to plan a deception and to carry it out, knowing good and evil, the ways of the world, before anyone eats from the tree. He knows God's motives for forbidding the fruit to the humans and has been in the inner circle, in the divine loop. And yet he is not God. He is the cleverest of all the "wild creatures that the Lord God made" (Gen 3:1). The snake, like the humans, is a creation of the Lord; he is an earth-dweller. His very desire to trick is peculiarly human as is Eve's desire to become wise, to test limits.

> The mediating function of the trickster explains that since its position is halfway between two polar terms he must retain something of that duality, namely an ambiguous and equivocal character. . .
> Not only can we account for the ambiguous character of the trickster, but we may also understand another property of mythical figures the world over, namely, that the same god may be endowed with contradictory

attributes; for instance, he may be *good* and *bad* at the
same time.

Lévi-Strauss, 1968:102–103

Or, we might add, he may be divine and human, wise and foolish, like the
beasts and like humankind. As a trickster, one who changes the status quo
through an act of trickery, and as a mediator, the snake leads in making
the passage from ideal to reality.

On one level, it is the humans he tricks, for he leads them to lose paradise, to be thrown out of the garden. The woman herself declares to God
that the snake deceived her. He draws her attention to the tree's desirabil-
ity and through clever speech leads her to take from God's tree. He uses
the truth—that the fruit jealously guarded by God gives one a godlike
wisdom—to trick her into changing her reality forever. On another level,
it is God who is tricked. Like the Greek gods who lose sole prerogative
over fire because of the machinations of Prometheus and who then, also
because of Prometheus, receive bones and little meat as sacrificial offering, so Yahweh loses exclusive claim to knowledge.

Like Zeus who punishes Prometheus—chaining him to a rock where
an eagle might tear at his liver, only to have it regenerate every night to
be torn again the next day—Yahweh punishes the trickster. He is cursed
to become a snake crawling on his belly, eating dust; he will bite humans'
heels and humans will crush his head. The snake is thus himself confined
to reptilian reality.

Cross-cultural comparison and more specifically structuralist suggestions of Lévi-Strauss thus lead to a deeper understanding of the role of
the snake in the patterns of narration and the patterns of meaning of Genesis 3.

An understanding of the roles of woman and man is further informed
by the field of women and folklore. The woman in Genesis 3 has been
portrayed as foolish and easily seduced or as temptress—sometimes as
both [see von Rad, "The one led astray becomes a temptress" (1959:87)].
Certainly later Western traditions blame woman for bringing death and
suffering into the world, a Pandora whose curiosity brings ruin (see, for
example *Gen. Rab.* 17:8). And while the pattern with which this chapter
began, ideal/prohibition broken/reality, also characterizes the Greek story
of Pandora, the Israelite version presents a much more independent-
minded, interesting, and complex protagonist who is neither a fool nor a
temptress but a culture bringer whose choices anticipate what most
makes us human. She attempts to debate with the snake when he mimics

God's prohibition to Adam. And when she eats from the tree, the narrator fully draws out for us her thinking: She sees that the tree is good to eat, desirable to the eyes, appealing to contemplate/to make wise. The play on *lĕhaśkîl* "to look upon"/"to make wise" gives special emphasis to the woman's interest in the tree. It is not merely a matter of curiosity but a more conscious desire to obtain wisdom. She, not her husband, is the protagonist of the story. Passively he takes what the woman offers him and eats. When the couple clothe themselves revealing their newfound sense of self, their awareness of sexual difference, and God confronts them with disobeying him and crossing his boundary dividing the divine and the human, the woman blames the snake for deceiving her. Childlike, quite comically, the man manages to accuse both the woman and God himself saying "That woman whom you gave to be with me, she gave to me from the tree and I ate." (3:12) For her part, the woman is consigned to a status under her husband. Her desire will be for him, but he will rule over her. Such is clearly the reality that the author of Genesis 3 considers to be the actual norm of his/her society.

Like the snake, woman is a mediator of sorts—she who becomes the embodiment of change, housing the life process itself, echoing in a seemingly routine way the creating of that first male progenitor. It is she who gestates earthlings who will live and die, she whose bloody discharge each month and after giving birth marks her as veritably chthonic—conditions associated in the priestly thread of Hebrew Scriptures with death and uncleanness. She thus contains within herself qualities of the earthly and the divine, of life and death (or the divine is perceived to house within himself the life-making qualities of woman). She, like the serpent, loses status after eating from the tree, for man now rules over her, but she, like the snake who sloughs its skin and was associated for this reason with immortality in the ancient Near East, retains and in fact comes overtly to manifest the capacity to make life continue. Thus she is named by her husband *Hawwah*, "The Mother of All Living Things." It is an honorable title, and Eve is to be regarded not as a symbol of death but as forbearer of a host of dynamic heroines in Genesis who serve as mediators, effect change, and whose power resides in the private realm of procreation.

3
The Ritual Narrative in Exodus 12

INTRODUCTION: EXODUS AS CREATION

If Eve's tale is imbedded in the larger story of the coming to be and ordering of the cosmos, Exodus 12, the text chosen as a case study in ritual, is imbedded in the larger narrative of the emergence of the people Israel. The writer responsible for the final form of Exodus was certainly conscious of echoing creation themes in his story of enslavement and emancipation. Moses the savior, born to be endangered like Oedipus, Cyrus, and so many other traditional heroes, is declared by his mother "to be good" (Ex 2:2) in the very words used by the creator deity to describe features of his cosmos in Genesis 1. Moses escapes in a basket called a *tēbāh*, the same word used for the ark in Noah's story of chaos and recreation in Genesis 6–9. The plagues that force Pharaoh to release the Hebrew slaves drag the Egyptians into chaos: blood is not contained in veins, but flows in rivers and streams; frogs appear in superfluity disrupting the balance of nature; beasts cross from their wild quarters to the settled land, disrupting the normal course of cosmogonic reality; darkness covers the day; and finally death, the ultimate form of chaos as sterility, strikes the Egyptian first born, rich and poor, old and young. The Hebrews, like Noah and his family, are not swept away by the chaos, being under divine protection. Then finally in Exodus 14–15, in another transformation of the chaos-to-cosmos theme, the Hebrews pass through the waters of the sea unscathed, their enemies defeated by God, ironicially overtaken by the flood of chaos which they themselves represent as the enemies of God's charges. Before the events of the Sea, told in the prose account of Exodus 14 and the archaic poem of chapter 15, comes the description of the Passover in chapter 12, now associated with ritual information pertaining to the first born in chapter 13.

An interesting question for biblical folklorists involves the ways in which recurring narrative patterns typical of traditionally composed literature come together in the edited corpora of the Hebrew Scriptures (see Niditch, 1986). Are those responsible for the final format of Scriptural collections participants in the traditional literary process and sensitive to such patterns, perhaps even using them as redactional principles, collecting materials of similar motifs and motif clusters or shaping disparate material in accordance with an overarching plan of patterning?

While such larger questions relating folklore to redaction and composition criticism are important, in this chapter we concentrate on Exodus 12 itself, its content and structure, its dominant symbols and themes, asking what the field of folklore can contribute to the study of this classic and fundamental biblical text. As in chapter 2, we will proceed first by outlining the major contours of discussions among biblical scholars, then provide an interpretation suggested by methodologies explored in the introduction.

REPRESENTATIVE SCHOLARLY CONCERNS

Representative major approaches in scholarship on Exodus 12 are as follows: Theodor Gaster's 1949 work (reprinted 1962) employing an updated and sophisticated version of Frazer's ethnographic methodology that relies upon collecting, cataloguing, and comparing folk motifs from around the world in order to understand the Israelite tradition; Martin Noth's 1959 (English ed., 1962) commentary which, like that of Hyatt (1971), is informed by source-critical assumptions about J,E, and P that are shared by most of the scholars in our soundings group (Noth:13–17); Brevard Childs's 1974 work that pays special attention to the final compositional or canonical form of the passage and its significance; and Nahum Sarna's more popularizing 1986 work that approaches Torah "not [as] a book of history, but [as] one that makes uses of historical data for didactic purposes, that is, for the inculcation of spiritual values and moral and ethical imperatives" (xi). Each scholar's emphasis is informed by his own methodological and theological interests, but major threads of discussion are remarkably similar: (1) Concern with J,E, and P in Exodus 12–13 and the relationship between the plagues account, the Passover, and regulations pertaining to the firstborn (Childs: 184; Hyatt: 137–44; Noth: 88–89, 92–93); (2) The suggestion that the Feast of Unleavened Bread was originally separate from the Pesach (Childs: 184; Hyatt: 136,187; Sarna: 87–89), the former frequently thought to stem from an agricultural celebration, the latter from a herdsman's spring festival (Noth: 88–89; Childs: 187,189; Sarna: 87–88); (3) An interest in setting the Passover ritual and its constituent symbols in terms of the ritual symbols of world religions and/or ancient Near Eastern traditions. In particular, scholars treat the sacrifice of the lamb in a quite functionalist way, as originally intended to "protect flocks" or "secure fertility" (Noth:95; Childs:188–89; Sarna:89; see also Hyatt:145; de Vaux:484–93). The offering was meant to appease the divine forces or win their protection. The blood served an apotropaic function, keeping away evil forces (Noth:89;90–91); (4) Above all, the Israelites are said to have transformed this "nomadic" or "seminomadic" or "primitive" rite, making it their own. As Sarna puts it, "Israel severed" the rite from its "mythical roots" (89) or historicized it (Noth:91; Childs:194). (See summary in Childs:188–89; also Gaster, 1949:16–25; Hyatt:145; Noth:95).

FOLKLORE AND BIBLICAL SCHOLARSHIP ON EXODUS 12

What would the folklorist do differently or how would she choose from among the basic orientations and interests outlined above?

The approaches most compatible with folkloristic interests would appear to be those of Childs. While recognizing the existence of sources and layers of tradition, he also emphasizes that the passage as now composed in the tradition has a validity, a wholeness, an artistry, and meaning as it stands (184–204). We are challenged to understand how Exodus 12 expresses the worldview and symbol system of those who put it together and of those who received it and found it meaningful. Childs also mentions the need to concern ourselves with the relationship between various parts of the tradition (191; 196–97). How are we to do so?

One way of approaching "the whole" is through the kind of cross-cultural study of symbols and ritual patterns engaged in by Gaster, expanded by attention to sociolinguistic, psychoanalytical, and anthropological concerns explored in the introduction above. And yet Childs—perhaps too dismissively—eschews "the usual patterns of comparative religions in which festivals, whether spring or fall, begin to look alike" (189). This is a criticism not only of Frazerism in new clothing but perhaps also of old-fashioned Semitics of the "Bibel und Babel" school. One can take a comparative approach and nevertheless concern oneself with the particulars of the tradition, and even with particular voices in the tradition. As folklorists, we seek to understand Exodus 12 in terms of the general (that is, the recurring symbols and combinations of symbols found in a cross section of cultures and within Israelite culture) and the specific (the special motifs and combinations of motifs found in Exodus 12). We are also particularly challenged by this passage which is neither a modern observer's report of a ritual nor a traditional narrative, but a description of ritual interwoven with its supposed template or model for the ritual. This model is presented as a narrative about threat and fear and the desire to escape, with overriding themes of group solidarity and the making of transitions. The writer of this material is quite conscious that he is describing a time of beginnings and how ritually (in Eliade's terms) to make a return to those beginnings—both through reading his narrative and through ritual enactment involving various significant symbolic actions and states. Like Exodus 1, the plagues account, and the exodus itself, Exodus 12 is creation literature.

Any reader of Exodus 12 must notice the sort of source-critical fissures to which scholars often point. First is the full description of the ritual, its symbols, and its significance by God (Ex 12:1–20). This description assumes the future tense and tells what the people should do and what will happen. Then the whole matter seems to be described again, this time by Moses who instructs the people (Ex 12:21–27). The resumption of a story assuming the past tense is found in v. 28 with a further reference in v. 42 to the wider implications of the events for the writer's own time. Finally the transition is made to a summary in vv. 43–51 about words of God to Moses concerning the composition of the celebrating community and other matters reemphasizing that Israel did as God commanded Moses, bringing events back to the "first Passover" when "on that very day the Lord brought out the people Israel from the land of Egypt in their hosts" (12:51). On the other hand, as Childs notes, the chapter as woven together has its own valid and logical structure and wholeness: God's instructions to Moses (vv. 1–20), Moses' repetition and elaboration to the people (vv. 21–27), the actual events (vv. 28–42), a summary about their significance and details for future observance (vv. 42–51). It is the viewpoint of this final whole that we seek to uncover and the ways in which it expresses a particular Israelite worldview, for the various parts of Exodus 12 reinforce one another and now participate in the formation of one myth. If these motifs of unleavened bread, sacrifice of the firstborn, and Passover offering did originally belong to separate ritual complexes, different groups, or different periods in the history of Israel, they now blend into one symbolic system, one meaning scheme, one story. What is this meaning scheme? The answer cannot be provided simply by reading the reasons for the holidays and the explanation of symbols offered in the text itself.

Turner has pointed to three "levels or fields of meaning" important in understanding the ritual symbols of a living culture. These three are equally relevant and helpful in exploring this story of ritual.

> Many ritual symbols are *multivocal* or *polysemous*, i.e., they stand for many objects, activities and relationships—there is not a one-to-one relationship between symbol and referent but a one-to-many relationship. Each major symbol has a "fan" or "spectrum" of referents (denotata and connotata), which tend to be interlinked by what is usually a simple mode of association, its very simplicity enabling it to interconnect a wide variety of referents. Some of the symbols we shall shortly consider have this polysemous character. I shall consider them firstly on the level of their *exegetical meaning*, secondly of their *operational meaning*, and thirdly of their *positional meaning*. The first level, briefly, represents the interpretations of my Ndembu informants—in this case of hunter-adepts—the second results from equating a symbol's meaning with its *use*, by noting what Ndembu do with it, and not only what they say about it, while the third level of meaning consists in examining a symbol's relationship to others belonging to the same complex or *gestalt* of symbols. I hope to show that this set of methodological tools has its uses in exposing to view the deeper layers of a society's system of values.
>
> Turner, 1967:254

The key symbols requiring explanation both singly and as parts of the ritual whole are the lamb and matters related to its selection, cooking, and eating; its blood; the unleavened bread; and the bitter herbs.

THE EXEGETICAL LEVEL

Exodus 12 is rich in native informants' explanations of what they are doing in the ritual, its meaning and significance. Turner's "exegetical level" is accessible if one views the "native informant" as the biblical writer who "got the last word," who put this narrative in its current form, who "tells" the story as he knows it.

One variety of exegesis overviews the meaning of the whole: "This month shall mark for you the beginning of months" (12:1). "It is the passover of the Lord, for I will pass through the land of Egypt that night, and I will strike down . . . execute judgments" (12:11,12) " . . . a day of remembrance . . . for on this very day I brought your hosts out . . ." (12:14, 17). "And when your children ask you . . . you shall say 'It is the *Passover* sacrifice to the Lord, for he *passed* over the houses of the Israelites in Egypt when he struck down the Egyptians, but our houses he spared'" (12:26,27). The etymology of the verb *psḥ* is, in fact, uncertain but it is clear that the Israelites for whom Exodus 12 was meaningful have given connotation to the verb meaning "pass by" or "save" or "skip over," "for that was a night of vigil" (12:42).

The occasion is clearly set up as marking a beginning, the first month of the year. Themes of salvation for Israel and of destruction for Egypt are emphasized as is God's "bringing out" of Israel. No surprises here. It is noteworthy that the striking down of the firstborn is treated as an "execution of justice," expressing from the perspective of biblical ethics a desire to portray the killing as just (see Niditch, 1993:25–27, 56–77). The Egyptians have made themselves deserving of judgment. The final plague is then not just a means to an end—a way finally to make pharaoh release those under his control—but punishment for his wrongdoing.

Specific comments by this native informant on specific symbols are also found. The blood is described in God's instructions as "a sign." "When I see the blood I will pass over. . . ." Why blood serves as a sign, why in Moses' instructions it is to be applied with a bunch of hyssop is not explained or exegeted and must be figured out at other levels. The unleavened bread has the most detailed "informant's" exegesis through implicit etiologies within the narrative. The dough is unleavened because the Egyptians rushed the Israelites out of the land and they scooped up their dough with their kneading bowls before leavening, so hasty were they to depart (vv. 34, 39). In this way, the feast of unleavened bread is integrally related to the Passover, the beginning of all months, and the rescue.

THE OPERATIONAL LEVEL

Although we cannot observe this ritual as actually practiced, the narrative describes what the people are instructed to do and said to do: a lamb without blemish is to be chosen (12:5), a year-old male from sheep or goats, one lamb for each household or if the household is too small, the lamb is to be obtained by two "closest neighbors" and shared (12:4). It is to be kept until the fourteenth day though obtained on the tenth, and slaughtered at twilight (12:6). All of the animal is to be eaten that night—leftovers are to be burned. It is interesting that no detailed instructions are given for the mode of slaughtering nor are specialized personnel involved. It is done by "the whole assembly of the congregation of Israel" (12:6; two words are used, *qĕhal* and *'ădat*) at the same time—presumably by a designated person within each household as described above. They are then to take from the blood and put it on the doorposts and lintels of the houses in which they eat the cooked meat (see 12:6, also repeated in Moses' instructions in 12:21–22 in which the blood is to be daubed with hyssop from a basin). Special instructions are given for the cooking and eating, including how the people should dress and act while eating. The lamb is to be roasted whole with its head, legs, and inner organs (12:8,9), eaten with unleavened bread and bitter herbs. It is to be eaten in a state of travel readiness, "loins girded," sandals on the feet, staff in hand, and hurriedly. These are instructions for "that night" but they apply also to the yearly repetition: "It is the Passover of the Lord" (12:12). No one is to go outside the house until morning (12:22).

Unleavened bread is to be eaten from the fourteenth until the twenty-first—seven days, the first and the last holy days encasing or surrounding the holiday as an inclusio. All Israelites and only members of the congregation of Israel, the circumcised, are to participate in the Passover.

The operational level of the ritual narrative takes the reader beyond the exegetical. The exegetical emphasizes a theme of us/them in terms of oppression, liberation, and the punishment of enemies, the theme of hasty departure and new beginnings sending important messages about Israel's self-definition as those whom Yahweh has chosen to save and about the exodus as a creation. The operational level of analysis greatly deepens one's understanding of the role of the ritual as narrated or redacted. Many of the symbols and symbolic actions connote wholeness, completeness, and a self-contained quality (see Gelber, 1989:35,42–44). The animal, as in all sacrifices, is to be without blemish. The sacrificial animal is to belong to a whole household or to two neighboring households, according to number of people required to consume all or most of it—again completeness is emphasized. Any leftovers are to be burned. Wholeness is emphasized by the seven-day feast of unleavened bread with its holy days at the opening and closing, by the fact that all stay inside their houses during the night's vigil, and by the specific requirement that only members of the Israelite community participate. The blood on the doorway demarcates those within from those without. Moreover, the animal is turned from raw to cooked in a most marked manner, roasted whole, entrails still intact, head upon the carcass; no bones are to be broken. Thus household by household, a whole community consumes all of a whole animal at the same time and becomes one—whole, separated, and circumscribed (on sacrifice as a means of defining membership in a group, see Jay, 1992:25,37,38,49,53). The seven-day eating of unleavened bread and avoidance of leaven further establishes a temporal and culinary wholeness as an entire community confines its diet to a certain type of bread for week. Like the eating of unleavened bread, the command to eat hastily explained at the exegetical or etiological level, as having to do with the escape, charges the ritual with an emotion of unrest, disruption, and imminent change. The bitter herbs are not explained at the exegetical level (in contrast to later Jewish exegeses; see also Ex 1:14).

What the Israelites are commanded to do and are said to do leads to the conclusion that the ritual has to do with transformation and with making whole. If the blood keeps the destroyer away, it also defines who is on the inside of the threshold (Gelber, 1989:25–26). Exodus 12 presumes that Israel is not a whole, describing them as they begin their journey as "about six hundred thousand men on foot, besides children . . . a mixed crowd also went up with them" (12:37,38). No group is a neat whole since it is composed of people of varying gender, age, and experience. At the operational level, the ritual actions of Exodus 12 serve to unite and to symbolize unity. The haste of eating, and, as Lévi-Strauss would tell us, the very act of cooking and consuming also emphasize transformation. In the Passover, the people are transformed into Israel.

THE POSITIONAL LEVEL: BLOOD, ROASTED WHOLE, BITTER HERBS, UNLEAVENED BREAD, HASTE

The "meal" of Exodus 12 is, in fact, very unlike a meal. The food is made rather unpalatable and basic. Some scholars draw comparisons with modern bedouin and suggest, for example, that the bitter herbs are a usual condiment for roast meat or that the unleavened cake is like pita bread, taming these symbols and making them ordinary reminders of a pastoral heritage. This is decidedly not the point of view of the writer of Exodus 12; the meat is prepared in a most unusual and unpalatable manner. The bitter herbs are not usual vegetable food. The matzo is not usual bread. On the spectrum from nature to culture, they are surely closer to the basic, natural side of the continuum. To understand more about these symbols we must now move beyond the operational to the positional level, setting the symbols and symbolic actions in a comparative context.

When Turner wrote of exploring symbols on the positional level, he was able to approach his work synchronically, studying a living, contemporary culture with its sets of associations between symbols. He could explore the position of "blood" as symbol in a Ndembu tribe in 1969, its relationship to substances such as milk and semen, its role in various ritual and narrative settings. For us the job becomes much more difficult. One might again emphasize for Exodus 12, as indeed for the Bible as a whole, that someone put the work together combining once disparate material. One might ask how the whole redacted work held unified meaning for an Israelite or Jew who accepted the current canon of the Hebrew Bible as a sacred set piece. On the other hand, an examination of the symbols of Exodus 12 at the positional level provides an exciting opportunity to do creative diachronic work. One asks not only how symbols of lamb, blood, unleavened bread, and bitter herbs are employed in Exodus 12 in ways comparable to and illustrated by other biblical texts, but also how their usage in Exodus 12 contrasts with other biblical cases. In this way, the uniqueness of Exodus 12 emerges, the better to approach questions about the "folk group" for whom this particular narration of ritual would have been meaningful.

LAMB ROASTED WHOLE

The term for "roasted" in Ex 12:8–9 is an unusual one: *ṣĕlî ʾēš*, "roasted in fire" (*ṣlh*: "to roast flesh"). The term is used as a verb in Isa 44:16, 19 to describe how an idolater uses the wood left over after building the image of his god. He builds a fire to roast himself some dinner. The text thus ridicules the idolater and his handiwork, reducing the sacred to the very mundane. So too in 1 Sam 2:15, the sons of Eli, greedy priests, demand raw meat from worshipers offering sacrifice to God, so they can cook it as they wish, again presumably in a mundane, profane, gluttonous fashion. They do not wish a portion of the boiled meat prepared in the course of the ritual but raw meat to prepare for themselves. The difficult passage in 1 Sam 2:15 possibly reflects a dispute about the proper way of preparing and consecrating meat in a sacrificial context. The roasters are treated as villains as in Isa 44:16. While the term *ṣlh* is unusual, the preparation of sacrifice by means of fire or the transference or transporting of sacrifice to God by means of immolation is of course found throughout Scripture. In theophanic contexts God or his power is frequently present in the fire. So Gideon's offering and that of Manoah and his wife are licked up in the flame (Judg 6:19–21; 13:15–20). In the latter case the angel himself returns to heaven in the flame of the offering presented by Samson's parents-to-be.

Offerings by fire are central to the baroque priestly sacrificial system described in Leviticus, as well as in less systematically presented and simpler acts of offering described for altar-building patriarchs, and in a host of other sacrificial acts that fall in the spectrum between these two. The ritual description in Exodus 12 is akin to priestly material in providing dates, a description of the animal chosen, its preparation, and so on and has been attributed in its final form to a priestly writer by modern scholarship (Hyatt:131–40). Certain aspects of the sacrifice are familiar from other sacrifices.

The šĕlāmîm or "wellbeing" sacrifices provided human beings an opportunity to eat meat. The officiating priest received the right thigh while the breast was shared by all the priests (Lev 7:31–34). The offerer received the rest. The "burnt offering" was entirely burned on the altar except for the hide which went to the priest (Lev 1; 7:8); other sacrifices, while forbidden to laity, were eaten by the priests (for example the "purification" or "sin" offering [6:22] [6:26 in English]; the "reparation" or "guilt" offering [Lev 7:1–6]). The requirement that the flesh of the sacrifice be eaten on the day it is offered is also found (the "thanksgiving" offering, a subset of wellbeing sacrifices [Lev 7:15], and the ordination offering [Ex 29:19–28; 31–34; Lev 8:22–29; 31–32]). The requirement that leftovers be burnt is also found (before morning for the thanksgiving sacrifice [Lev 7:15]; on the third day for votive and free will "wellbeing offerings" [Lev 7:17]; see also the ordination offering [Ex 29:34; Lev 8:32]).

There are, however, significant differences between the Passover sacrifice described in Exodus 12 and all others. These differences provide important hints about its positional meaning in a larger Israelite symbol system, and perhaps in a trajectory of Israelite cultural history.

ROASTING WHOLE

The most immediately noticed difference between this sacrifice, which provides an opportunity for a meal, and others is the way the animal is prepared for the altar. The stated way to prepare an offering in priestly texts involves slaughter, flaying, cutting up into parts, and the careful arrangement on the altar of what is to be offered by fire. The entrails and legs are to be washed with water. This is true of the totally burnt offering (Lev 1:3–9) and of those offerings in which flaying and cutting allow for a selected portion to go to the priest, certain other portions to be dedicated to God, and so on (see the description of the preparation of the well-being offering in Lev 9:18–21). The Passover sacrifice, however, is roasted whole with head, legs, and inner organs. Indeed for those accustomed to more careful and distributive preparations, the animal with head and entrails intact might seem a quite unappetizing meal. It is certainly not the way food is extracted from the sacrifice, but there is more. When a portion of a sacrificial animal is allowed as food for human beings, it is not roasted in fire, but boiled. God's offering is burnt in the fire, but the portion allowed humans is boiled. Thus, concerning the ordination offering, of which the priests are allowed a portion, Moses tells Aaron to "boil the flesh at the entrance of the tent of meeting and eat it there" (Lev 8:31). The sin offering allowed to the priests is boiled (Lev 6:21 [6:28 in the English]). Ezekiel's vision of the rebuilt temple allows for kitchens where those who serve at the temple shall boil the sacrifices of their people (Ezek 46:20,24). "The priest shall take the shoulder of the ram when it is boiled" (Num 6:19; see also Ex 29:31; Zech 14:21; 1 Sam 2:13). God's food is cooked with fire, transferring it to the deity with pleasing odor. Human's food is prepared more indirectly, boiled in water in a pot, heated by the fire.

As Marcel Detienne has pointed out, modes of cooking a sacrifice— boiling or roasting (or both in a particular order)—are significant cultural markers (see also Jay:25,53). In his study of classical Greek tradition, Detienne explores why in Dionysian sacrificial ritual the meat is boiled and then roasted whereas normal sacrificial practice is to roast and then boil (1977b:173). In our case the question is: Given that God's portion is normally burned and humans' portion boiled, why in the Passover sacrifice, is human food roasted in fire?

What distinguishes fired meat from boiled meat? Fire is a more direct, more basic, and more primitive way of cooking requiring only fire and the meat—perhaps a stick for a spit. Boiling requires a pot made by human invention; it is an indirect, more complicated and acculturated means of food preparation (Lévi-Strauss, 1978:479–80). Roasting in fire is an intermediate stage between "the raw and the cooked." A mediating form of food preparation, the burning of meat, sends it up to God, a God who often appears in Israelite contexts in the wild, by a river, or in the wilderness—in pure places unsullied by human invention and society. One must not overdraw the distinction between nature and culture, "raw" and "cooked," implied by the above line of reasoning. All ritual is intricately inventive and cultural. Nevertheless in this narrative of ritual action, Israelites substitute for some of the usual or normal particulars of meat eating more natural food that is usually reserved for God, and in the process they make themselves intermediaries, cementing crucial relationships in the very process of making a transition.

SHARING GOD'S FOOD

Through the consumption of the whole lamb roasted by fire, Israelites, family by family, in a most democratized, decentralized fashion, partake of a meal with God. The sacred food is not only allowed to them; they are required to eat it. Like the elders and Moses transported to the heavenly realm to eat and drink with God (Ex 24:9–11), Israelites, through preparation and consumption of God's food, enter a sacred space within their own homes, to eat and drink with God. Eating roasted meat instead of boiled thus serves to mark a fellowship between Israel and God, a confirmation of their close relationship forged in the exodus. Israel is God's people, God, Israel's god.

SHARING THE WHOLE: THE PEOPLE AS WHOLE

Study at the positional level further explains how unity is symbolized and effected in the shared lamb, roasted whole in fire, and completely consumed, enclosed family by enclosed family. The lamb thus prepared is basic food, primitive food, stripped bare, unfancy food. Together with the bitter herbs and unadorned unleavened cakes it is the food of the ritual passenger. After commenting briefly on bitter herbs and matzot, we will look more closely at rites of passage. Relevant in this context are the ways anthropologists describe the relationship between those undergoing ritual transitions and Turner's suggestions concerning symbolizations of that state of sharing and community.

BITTER HERBS: NATURE VERSUS CULTURE AND UNUSUAL FOOD

Many scholars suggest that the bitter herbs are a condiment of sorts that "nomadics" or herdsmen would have enjoyed with their meat. Like the meat prepared by fire, however, the herbs are not usual food. A positional analysis proves quite the contrary. Most of the terms stemming from the root and other biblical contexts for these terms suggest an unpleasant sort of bitterness (see BDB: 600–601). The only exception is the word *mōr*, "myrrh," an aromatic fragrance. But *mĕrērāh* is "gall"; *mĕrōrāh*, "a bitter thing, gall, poison." The only non-Passover context for the *mārōr* of Ex 12:8 is in the ironic sarcasm of Lam 3:15, "He has satisfied me with bitterness/And satiated me with wormwood." Like the whole roasted lamb, the herbs are closer to the nature side of the nature/culture continuum—basic, even base—unappetizing for human consumption but required of all Israelites, a shared experience among Israelites, household by household. Vegetation, uncooked food of the earth, and God's food, cooked with fire, provide the food of ritual passengers.

THE UNLEAVENED BREAD

The unleavened cakes, like offerings of fired flesh, are found in various sacrificial contexts (Lev 7:12; 6:8–10 [vv. 15–17 in the English]; 2 Kings 23:9). In the grain offering, the flour of the cakes is prepared with oil and aromatics in a special way (Lev 6:8–9 [6:15–16 in the English]). Plain cakes are spread with oil as part of the sacrifice of well-being (Lev 7:12). The grain offering, like the roasted flesh, is God's food (Lev 6:7–9 [6:14–15 in the English]). Unleavened cakes are taken up in flames by God in Judg 6:19–22, Gideon's theophanic experience. Elsewhere, however, plain unleavened cakes are treated as simple, quickly prepared, basic fare for people (such as what the woman of Endor prepares for Saul in 1 Sam 28:24). On one level, apart from the Passover tale, they are "the bread of affliction," literally "poor bread," bread of poverty (see Deut 16:3 concerning Passover unleavened bread). In partaking of matzot for a week, the Israelites eat what is most basic and natural—for leavening requires more preparation and is an acculturated, more complex way of preparing food—but also what is sometimes God's food. Positionally, matzot are thus between *mārōr*—no human's food—and roasted lamb—God's exclusive purview—making the three the perfect sandwich for ritual passengers changing status and forging relationships.

Many scholars suggest that leaven is avoided in the hypothesized original "feast of unleavened bread" and in the Passover reported in Exodus 12 because to leaven is to ferment and is to consume what is corruptible and decaying. This is why, they suggest, the meat must be consumed in one night and not left over. The informant's exegesis here, however, tallies beautifully with the positional study. The matzot are fast food on some level, not to be savored and enjoyed but to be hastily and solemnly consumed—special food, circumscribed nonfood, food out of which shared experiences are forged.

THE LIMINALS IN A RITE OF PASSAGE

Once again studies of ritual rites of passage are relevant. During these ritual formalizations of changes in social status from youth to adulthood, virginity to marriage, and so on, those undergoing the same transition become a close-knit group sharing the experience of transformation. The rite involves a symbolic separation from present status—often a physical removal to a special location and a stay for a certain length of time in a betwixt and between condition while the old status is stripped away. As discussed in chapter 2, such in-between transition conditions in which the passenger prepares himself or herself for a new status are often symbolized by disguises, special clothing, or the removal of all clothing. In traditional cultures, one not only is what one wears or does not wear but also what one eats. The consumption of fired meat, bitter herbs, and unleavened bread is an emersion into nature, a partaking of the earthy and the divine that bonds the eaters with each other as initiates in a rite of passage, all eating the same thing and at the same time in unity, each contained by household, marked and sealed by the lamb's blood on doorpost and lintel.

BLOOD ON THE POSITIONAL LEVEL

Transitions are dangerous. God the destroyer is abroad during the Passover night. Hence modern scholars and the native exegetes' suggestion that the blood is an apotropaic that keeps the destroyer away—the Israelites would say that it is a sign, a "red flag" that the house is Israelite and not Egyptian. All in this world of Israelite and non-Israelite face changes. The relationship between free and enslaved will be altered as the Israelites become free and, in fact, acquire Egyptian wealth. The Egyptians are robbed of their finery and of their dearest possessions, their firstborn children. The blood separates Egyptian from Israelite and marks the spaces where the Israelites' new identity is being forged. A Frazerian might say that it is also a time of seasonal transition. It is, after all, the beginning of spring. The positional significance of blood, however, in the larger Hebrew Scriptures is especially informative.

The daubing of blood of an animal sacrifice in other Israelite rituals is an act of purifying, effecting a transition from unclean to clean status, allowing the location (such as an altar) or a person (such as a cured leper) once again to be in touch with the sacred. The blood, red like the earth its soundalike, ruddy like humans or earthlings, also its soundalike, is what makes us human. It is also the source of God-given life, forbidden as food because the life is in it (Lev 17:11; Deut 12:23). It is then stuff of the spirit as well, another of these multivocal symbols about which Turner writes that helps to mediate between Israel's former and future status and that emphasizes the people's shared humanity while at the same time placing them in God's house.

DEMOCRATIZATION?

Having explored the Passover ritual and its constituent symbols at various levels, we are now prepared to ask whose worldview these symbols reflect. Clearly the themes of unity and wholeness and the theme of transformation or passage from slavery to liberation are as ancient as Israel and relevant to current Jewish celebration as well. The more reliable way of approaching questions of author and audience is the comparative positional analysis that reveals the special significance of burning the meat by fire and eating in the blood-purified confines of the household. The complete absence of priestly roles in the preparation of the animal, the sanctification by blood of ordinary homes, and the people's consumption of food burned in fire like God's food suggests a democratized ritual. These people sharing whole lambs, household by household, are a group of equals. The lamb is not divided before cooking. No hierarchy is established, marked by who receives which portion of meat.

It seems, therefore, unlikely that the account in Exodus 12 is the work of Judean priests of the monarchic period, serving in the central and centralizing sanctuary in Jerusalem, fully conscious of and protective of their own status as mediators between God and Israel. From those in Israel who uphold a centralizing ideal come what are essentially corrections or regularizations of the household-based Passover, rendering the Passover less subversive. The instructions in Deuteronomy 16 for the Passover celebration, for example, specify that the Passover sacrifice be offered "at the place that the Lord will choose as a dwelling for his name" (16:2,5–6). As in Deut 12:14, this is technical language for the Jerusalem sanctuary where God's name has come to dwell. Thus Passover becomes a pilgrimage festival. Rather than contain each family in its own house in its own community, the sacrifice is *not* to be offered "within any of your towns"; the towns and home must be left to sacrifice with other Israelites at a central sacred place—the Jerusalem Temple. Moreover, the meat to be eaten "at the place that the Lord will choose" is to be "boiled." (The term *bšl* is used, indicating the typical mode of preparation of food to be consumed by humans, expressly forbidden in Exodus 12.) Thus Passover is brought into line with other sacrificial feasts in the time of the Temple, as the pro-centralization voice in Deuteronomy 16 would represent it. Interestingly this voice calls the Israelites' homes "tents." They are to return to their "tents" the next day, evoking the wilderness setting of the book of Deuteronomy. The "place chosen" is presumably the tabernacle and the period is that of wilderness wanderings. This is an immersion into the setting of Deuteronomy that belies the passage's Temple period date. The sacrificial ritual has been tamed; humans are not enjoined to eat God's food, nor are their own homes turned into sacred spaces marked by blood. Yet is Deuteronomy 16 a later text than Exodus 12? Perhaps, but perhaps Deuteronomy 16 reflects an alternate but contemporaneous tradition, an alternate view of the proper constellation of symbols that make for the celebration of the exodus, a tradition tied to a quite hierarchical and worship-centralizing view whereas Exodus 12 reflects the attitude expressed in Ex 19:6 "but you shall be for me a kingdom of priests and a holy nation."

2 Chronicles 30—the story of Hezekiah's celebration of Passover—provides another view of the Passover. This Passover is a celebration in the substitute second month (see Num 9:9–14) because the priests need the time to sanctify themselves in sufficient numbers and the people need time to gather in Jerusalem. The people "had not been doing it in great numbers" (celebrating the Passover as it is written) and Hezekiah issues a proclamation to come and keep the Passover (2 Chron 30:5). Celebrating the Passover thus becomes a way to return to God (2 Chron 30:6–9). All, of course, takes place in Jerusalem. Levites slaughter the lamb for many of the people who are not in a state of ritual purity. The eating of the lamb is mentioned, but not the mode of cooking. The whole matter is smoothed over. Of greater interest for our present purpose is 2 Chron 35—Josiah's Passover, celebrated in the "holy place" "according to the groupings of the ancestral houses," with Levites positioned for each division of an ancestral house (35:5). In this way, the priestly establishment, imagined typically by the Chronicler to involve an active and inclusive role for the Levites, is intertwined with the allowance that Passover is celebrated household by household. Accommodation is thus made for these two threads—"the word of the Lord by Moses" in Exodus 12 (2 Chron 35:6) and the centralization of the cult. The Levites appear to slaughter the Passover lamb, the priests dash (*zrq*) the blood (2 Chron 35:11) as in offerings of well-being (Lev 3:2) and in burnt offerings (Lev 1:5). The Passover lamb is skinned by the Levites (2 Chron 35:11), as is usual for other sacrifices but not enjoined in Exodus 12 where the animal

is roasted whole. Thus another important aspect of the symbolism of Exodus 12 is altered as the Passover looks much like other offerings. 2 Chron 35:13 juxtaposes the roasting of the lamb with the boiling of holy offerings in pots, kettles, and casseroles—offerings that are then quickly delivered to all the people. Thus no mention is made of the actual eating of the Passover lamb—a plethora of other offerings, portions of which are boiled and eaten in the usual way, confuse or defuse issues implicit in eating God's special food.

POSITIONAL READINGS AS REDACTION CRITICISM

Do versions of the Passover—especially references to the way the lamb is prepared in Deuteronomy 16—reflect a change over time from decentralized to centralized modes of celebrating the Passover? Alternatively, is Exodus 12 a late text, a reading back into earliest times, a time of beginnings, a home by home sort of marking of the Passover in the absence of a temple and centralized cult? This would date Exodus 12 to a period between 586 and 520 B.C.E. More likely, Exodus 12 is ritually meaningful to a group that allows for ritual consumption of meat in the home—at least at the Passover festival—and that pictures the union between God and Israel as possible at such decentralized settings. 2 Chron 35 especially attempts to harmonize these alternate conceptions of the Passover or safely to fence the home-based one within the contours of the centralized temple cult. Exodus 12 is retained in Hebrew Scriptures because it assumes the role of an account of the first Passover (Hyatt [133] suggests "P" is "reverting . . . to the primitive custom"). For narrative purposes it is set in olden times before the existence of the temple, but it is reasonable to assume that for large numbers of Israelites this was the Passover to which they returned annually through ritual, a celebration subversive to those believing in a centralizing ideal, to those who generally have the last word in the Hebrew Bible.

CONCLUSIONS

A symbolic analysis of Exodus 12 and related texts inspired by the work of cultural anthropologist Turner, whose studies of myth and ritual have been most influential in the field of folklore, leads to a fascinating exercise in tradition-history. In the process have been revealed tensions and attempts to harmonize tensions in essential aspects of Israelite religion.

4
Folklore and Wisdom:
Mashal as an Ethnic Genre

INTRODUCTION: EARLIER WORK

Issues in proverbs provide a third case study in Bible and folklore. The excellent work of Claudia V. Camp, James Crenshaw, Carole Fontaine, Galit Hasan-Rokem, Raymond Van Leeuwen and others has already brought the field of folklore and biblical material together in richly insightful ways.

As Fontaine describes the work that precedes her own, trends in the study of biblical proverbs parallel many of those that have characterized scholarship on Genesis 3 and Exodus 12: (1) the redactional-critical interest underscored by Otto Eissfeldt's seminal work that explores the various applications of the term *mashal* and the relation between supposedly simpler and briefer folk sayings and more elaborate and sophisticated wisdom sayings (see discussion and critical review by Fontaine; Crenshaw, 1976:14,24,26); (2) the relation of biblical proverbs to other ancient Near Eastern proverbs (Crenshaw, 1976:5–9); (3) the locus and use of proverb collections in wisdom schools and/or the origins and functions of sayings in a clan or tribal setting (see Crenshaw, 1976:16,21–22; Fontaine's summary:25); (4) definition of the characteristics of form and content in various sorts of biblical proverbs (see Fontaine:24–25; Crenshaw's review, 1976:14–15).

FOLKLORISTS' QUESTIONS

Folklorists are also interested in versions of all of these questions: the ways in which oral sayings are included in written literary works and the transformations that take place (Mieder,1974); the defining of the genre proverb (Dundes, 1975; Abrahams, 1972b:119–22; Seitel:125); cross-cultural comparison of proverbs (Hasan-Rokem, 1990); questions about the function, setting, and form of proverbs in particular folk groups (Jason,1971b; Holbek, 1970; Messenger).

Other threads of modern folklore scholarship that are of special interest to Fontaine and other experts on biblical wisdom who are aware of folklore methodologies fall under the headings of form and function. Folklorists such as Dundes have explored the form of the proverb structurally, suggesting that the genre is defined most basically as a "topic" and a "comment" or a combination of topics and comments. Proverbial structure may be equational: "Haste (topic) makes waste (comment)"; "Time (topic) is money (comment)"; or contrastive: "Two wrongs don't make a right"; "Hindsight is better than foresight" (Dundes, 1975; in Mieder and Dundes, 1981:55); and more or less ornate. "A bird in hand (topic and comment) is worth two in the bush (topic and comment)" is, for example, a multidescriptive element proverb that contrasts one bird with two (see Dundes, in Mieder and Dundes, 1981: 52).

Dundes's underlying structure of topic/comment is not always as neatly applied to multidescriptive proverbs as he implies. As Van Leeuwen has shown, the second half of an equational or oppositional multidescriptive proverb such as the phrase "first fired" in the saying "last hired/first fired" might be viewed at a "deep" structural level of analysis as the comment, and not a topic and comment. While topic/comment may be a valid means of linguistic, syntactic analysis indicating, for example, a subject and modifier for each segment of a proverb, it may not be the most semantically meaningful model. While Dundes analyzes the whole proverb cited above as follows: hired/fired: topics; last/first: comments, one might view the topic as "last hired" and the comment as "first fired" (see examples, discussion, and definition of topic/comment in Van Leeuwen, 1988:47–51). In any event, Dundes's structuralist suggestions and those of others discussed and influenced by him help to provide methodological handles for the study of any culture's proverbs.

Such an approach, for example, helps to unravel the worldview of the author of Ecclesiastes who, as Robert Gordis has noted in a classic article, appears to quote or to parody the sort of material or the actual sayings found in the book of Proverbs. See, for example, in Eccl 1:18 examples of a typical saying structure used in two proverbs, set up as the lines in a bicolon.

> In much wisdom is much vexation.
> He who increases knowledge increases pain.

The topic and comment in the first colon are synonyms of the topic and comment in the other: "wisdom" and "knowledge," "vexation" and "pain." Here we are using Van Leeuwen's version of Dundes's topic/comment. Outlining the proverbs' structure allows one to see the radical and ironic equation made by an author between tradition's accepted good—"wisdom/knowledge"— and the supposed emotions and results of anti-wisdom—"vexation/pain." The author uses a typical (perhaps universal) saying structure to challenge his own and his audience's learned belief system. The ear and the mind expect different "fill in the blanks" than the ones offered in Eccl 1:18, and thus instead of reinforcing the status quo, the sayings challenge it. It is the use of a structural pattern that so often supports the status quo that makes the message in Ecclesiastes purposefully confusing, provocative, and subversive.

Similarly in Eccl 7:1, the author employs a saying structure and the sort of content found also in Prov 22:1:

> Better a good reputation than fine oil (Eccl 7:1).
> Preferred is a reputation than great wealth (Prov 22:1).

In Eccl 7:1, this saying is juxtaposed with a radical version: "And the day of death than the day of birth." Prov 22:1, however, continues in a most expected way: "Than silver and gold is favor better." Again it is the underlying structure, and the authors' and the receivers' consciousness of it, that gives Eccl 7:1 its punch, its surprise, and that makes the reader pause.

Another important contribution of folklorists involves the emphasis they place on context for rendering the proverb meaningful. What, for example, are the various ways the very same proverb can be understood by various groups or individuals depending upon the particular tone of the speaker, the situation in which speaker and audience find themselves, the relationship between the two, or the cultural expectations they share. Barbara Kirshenblatt-Gimblett (1973) provides two interesting cases showing in one study how the saying "money talks" can be used to convey a wide range of varying emotions, tones, and intents depending upon the situational context and the relative status of speaker and receiver. In a second study, she shows how, depending on cultural referents, the saying, "A rolling stone gathers no moss" can be understood as having either a positive assessment or "comment" on the topic (a rolling stone), ("If you keep busy and moving you won't go stale, flabby or the like") or a negative one ("If you keep moving, you'll never establish roots").

Roger Abrahams shows further how in interpersonal situations proverbs can be used to assert status diplomatically, to mediate disputes, to relieve tension, or to criticize without angering the person the proverb-quoter believes to be in the wrong (1968:150–52). A person of lower status, for example, may criticize one who has power over him or her indirectly through the use of a proverb, thereby avoiding direct confrontation. Alternatively, a parent may correct a child and avoid a direct dressing down by quoting an appropriate proverb. Combining structural and sociological interests, Seitel provides a model for understanding the ranges of a proverb's possible meanings in various contexts (see also Kirshenblatt-Gimblett, 1973).

Attention to context is important not only in exploring interpersonal situations and various oral settings, but also in understanding intertextual relationships in the wisdom corpus. One learns much, for example, when tracing what happens when a saying that was probably used in oral settings is placed in various bookish contexts. The transformations in meaning and message are fascinating indicators of their bookish users' worldviews. For example, the relationship between Prov 26:27 and Eccl 10:8 is revealing (see also Prov 28:10; Ps 7:15–16; Job 4:8; Ps 9:15). In Prov 26:27 the saying is surrounded by sayings on deception (see vv. 24–26, 28 concerning the "lying tongue" and "smooth mouth") and the listener is assured that he who sows deceptions and hatred will be "hoisted by his own pitard." "Whoever digs a pit will fall into it/Whoever rolls a stone, upon him it will return" (kōreh šaḥat bāh yippōl)." The author of Eccl 10:8, however, places a variation on the same saying (using other equivalent Hebrew terms for "dig" and "pit" [ḥōper gûmmāṣ bô yippôl]), in the midst of a series of "on-the-job" accidents that prove that things often do not turn out the way they are supposed to. In Ecclesiastes the saying's context deals with the world of social rank gone awry—slaves on horseback, princes on foot (10:7), with wisdom's mercenary promises for success disproven: folly set in high places/wealthy in a low place (10:6). The consequences of one's actions are unpredictable and often a task turns out to be thankless. Thus quite literally:

> He who digs a pit, will fall into it.
> He who breaks through a wall, a snake will bite him.
> He who quarries rocks will be hurt by them.
> He who splits logs will be endangered by them.
>
> Eccl 10:8–9

The two apparently equivalent sayings thus turn out to have very different messages. One recommends a particular ethical stance—honesty—and insists that justice will be served upon the deceiver and ultimately that the "system" is just and the world orderly. The other describes the lack of order in the world, the lack of predictability, in a way that encourages a virtual paralysis. Shall I eat a peach? It probably will be rotten and make my hands sticky anyway. In short, context is essential to understanding the saying, be the context oral-traditional or literary.

FONTAINE, CAMP, AND PROVERBS: FOLKLORISTIC INTERESTS

Attention to the structural composition of the proverb and concern with cultural and literary contexts and particular interpersonal contexts inform the work of Fontaine and Camp (see also Fontaine-Camp; Darr) who explore the form and possible meanings of proverbs that are set in biblical narratives. Fontaine acknowledges that the biblical situations in which the proverbs are found cannot be regarded as having taken place as narrated or to have taken place at all; these narratives contain castings of characters, situations, and plots that tell about events as they might have been or should have been from the author's point of view, or as tradition holds them to have been. They are composed by authors shaping their tales in accordance with certain conventions, stamping them with the special concerns and influences of their own times and personalities. Nevertheless, the creative work of these authors, suggests Fontaine, indicates the sort of actual settings in which proverbs might have been used or at the least that Israelite audiences appreciated and understood stories in which proverbs serve a range of sociolinguisitc functions such as mediating disputes.

Camp has added a feminist dimension to her study of proverbs, folklore, and the Bible. She has explored the persona of Woman Wisdom and the Strange Woman of Proverbs 1–9, those larger-than-life figures associated in the Israelite tradition with taking advice or breaking advice of the wisdom tradition (1985). She has also explored the connection between wise women, mediation as a social function, and proverbial lore (1990). Thus the wise woman of Tekoa, speaking in the rhetoric of proverbs, convinces David to take back his son the prince Absalom (2 Sam 14:1–20). Abigail furthers her own career and prevents the destruction of her husband's household by the younger bandit leader David (1 Sam 25:2–42). Woman, the connector of generations and of in-marrying groups, thus becomes a professional mediator.

ETHNIC GENRES AND LITERARY CONTEXTS

My own case study in the Bible, proverbs, and folklore opens another very basic avenue for exploration. How does one define and understand

71

the Israelite term *mashal*? Is the *mashal* a meaningful literary category in Israelite tradition? Does a genre recognized among the Israelites lie behind the Bible's many invocations of the term? Here one is building on the classic study of the *mashal* by Eissfeldt, and upon later works by A. R. Johnson, William McKane, George Landes, A. S. Herbert, Timothy Polk, and others. The folkloristic perspective asks how and why proverbs do not have a term all their own in ancient Israel, but are grouped with an array of other types of literature. That is, while we may call Ezek 16:44, "like mother/like daughter," a proverb, an Israelite calls it the same thing as Ezek 17:2ff., which we might call a parable, or Num 23:7ff. which we might call an oracle.

It may be valid for heuristic purposes to use our own culture's terminology or to superimpose our term "proverb" on a corpus of biblical material. Fontaine's definition of "proverb" (1982:65), Hasan-Rokem's definition (1990:108, 1982:11), and that of Dundes (1975) all work for a wide range of sayings from various cultures. Although their emphases on structure, context, theme, and function may differ and although they might take issue with how best to describe the phenomenon, it is understandable why and how biblical proverbs might fit the definitions these scholars have developed. But Ben-Amos (1992a) encourages us to ask the question from a different perspective. Why do Israelite writings include proverbs within an apparently wider category? How do Israelites implicitly define that category and what does it say about them, their aesthetics, and their worldview? Words matter. As Ben-Amos has written in a fascinating study of the biblical miracle (1992a; see also 1992b:18), if the Israelites do not have a specific term for the phenomenon scholars have been identifying as a miracle, then do they share the concept of miracle as we understand it? Was "miracle" a meaningful category of experience and of literature for Israelites or have we superimposed our notion of miracle on these biblical accounts (1992a:42)? In the case of the *mashal* we do find a term, sometimes applied to sayings like our proverbs but also applied to other types of material. There is, then, among Israelites apparently an ethnic genre called the *mashal*. How might Israelites have delineated and defined this category of literature, and what does its definition say about them aesthetically and intellectually?

SYNCHRONIC VERSUS DIACHRONIC

One might respond to suggestions that we have failed to appreciate a biblical ethnic genre and that we have superimposed our concept of proverb on biblical sayings that are called *mashal* by pointing out that Israelites of various periods and settings did not always use the term *mashal* in the same way, or refer to the same thing when they used the term. That is, one might conclude that the *mashal* is not one definable genre in the Hebrew Bible (see, for example, Mowry:651 and the discussion in Suter:194–5). The case for the diachronic, even evolutionary understanding of *mashal* is made by Eissfeldt. Etymologically, he notes the root *mšl* means "to be similar." The term *mashal* derived from the root was applied to a saying form, the oral folk proverb, and a narrative form, the similitude. As the oral and implicitly more primitive stage of Israelite literatures gives way to the written stage, the term *mashal* is then applied to various genres such as the longer wisdom saying and the taunt (see also Landes:140). Finally, in a line of development from wisdom sayings, *mashal* is applied to the genre "instruction" which need not look proverbial at all. From the similitude the term is applied to oracular discourse (Eissfeldt: 29–44). The instruction and the oracular discourse are thus far removed from the original concept of "being similar." *Mashal* means something different in Ezek 24:3 than it does in Job 27:1; 29:1; and 1 Sam 24:14 (v. 13 in English). Differing "folk groups" may have used the term differently. The prophet who declares that people call him *měmaššēl mě-šālîm*: "a crafter of proverbs" in Ezek 21:5 (20:49 in English) may mean something different from the author who describes Koheleth similarly in Eccl 12:9, different also from the weaver of *mashal* in Num 21:27 who appears to cite a saying about a legendary event.

And yet there is evidence in the Book of Ezekiel that the term *mashal* was understood at least in one period and one setting to mean proverb (in our sense) in Ezek 16:44 ("Like mother/like daughter) and 18:2 ("The parents eat sour grapes/the children's teeth are set on edge"); to mean allegory or similitude, or whatever equally imprecise term from our culture we wish to impose in Ezek 17:2 (the eagle tale); and to mean an oracle, perhaps even an incantation of sorts, in Ezek 24:3. Is something different meant each time the term *mashal* is used in Ezekiel? That seems unlikely. Polk also turns to Ezekiel and accepts that a single category, *mashal*, includes all the cases in which the term is used in that work as does Suter who states that "any attempt to define *māšāl* . . . must take seriously its application to a variety of forms. The biblical writers recognize all of these forms as belonging to a family and do not develop a terminology that distinguishes between them" (196).

Examples from the cultures studied by Finnegan offer some interesting ethnolinguistic parallels to the term *mashal* as used by Ezekiel and in the wider Israelite tradition.

The Fulani *mallol* for instance means not only a proverb but also allusion in general. . . . Similarly with the Kamba term *ndimo*. This does not exactly correspond to our term 'proverb' but is its nearest equivalent, and really means a dark saying or metaphorical wording, a sort of secret and allusive language. . . Proverbs are not always distinguished by a special term from other categories of verbal art. The Nyanja *mwambi*, for instance, refers to story, riddle, or proverb, the Ganda *olugero* means, among other things a saying, a story, a proverb, and a parable . . . . Limba *mb'r'* refers to story, riddle, and parable as well as to sayings which we might term proverbs, while the Fulani *tindol* can mean not only a popular moral story but also a proverb or maxim.

Finnegan, 1970:390–91

GENERAL REFERENCES TO *MASHAL*

A first step in resolving the question is to see how the term *mashal* is used either without reference to a particular saying or parable or in an extended rubric that comments on the phenomenon of *mashal* itself. People presumably understood what an Israelite author meant when mentioning the *mashal*, even when the term is not used to introduce an example or examples of the genre. References to the *mashal* (pl.) of Solomon preserved in the Book of Proverbs, are rubrics appearing to refer to material that follows them, but this biblical book contains a mixed bag of literature and thus does not help to focus on a definition of the genre. In other references, the parallel terms of biblical poetry provide better opportunities for understanding what was meant by *mashal*, although no precise definitions are offered.

> Let the wise person listen and increase received knowledge (*leqaḥ*)
> Let the intelligent person acquire guidance.
> To understand a *mashal* and oblique speech [an enigma],
> The words of the wise and their obscure speech [riddles].
> Prov 1:5–6

First, the *mashal* is among things "received," "acquired," passed on. And associated with it are forms of knowledge that are rooted in words meaning indirect or oblique *mĕlîṣāh*, related to the Arabic "turn aside"; *hîdāh*, related to the Arabic "turn aside, avoid".

Ps 78:2–5 provides an interesting extended comment on *mashal*.

> I will open my mouth with a *mashal*
> I will pour forth obscure speech (*hîdôt*, riddles) from ancient times.
> That which we have listened to and known
> And that our ancestors told us.
> We will not hide [them] from their children
> To the coming generation will we talk-story,
> The praiseworthy deeds of the Lord and his might,
> His wonders that he has done.

Here *mashal* is even more overtly associated with passing down through generations, historical traditions, and inherited knowledge (see also Ps 78:5–8 on teaching and knowing). The obscure speech (riddle) word is associated here with *mashal* as is the image of telling stories of God's wondrous deeds, themselves mysterious and inexplicable by ordinary rational human agency (Ben-Amos, 1992a). Verses 9–72 are a poetic tour through the high points of Israelite tradition, including miraculous rescues and Israelite shortcomings as a nation of ingrates.

Ps 49:5 (v. 4 in the English) associates the *mashal* with the *hîdah*, and the "opening up" of the latter with music. Eccl 12:9 describes Koheleth the wise man as "weighing" or "testing" or "proving," (*'zn*), "searching out" (*hqr*), and "making straight" (*tqn*; that is, "arranging" or "figuring out the indirect") many *mashal*'s.

> Your memorials (from *zkr*, "to remember") are *mashal*'s
> of dust/Your [memorial] mounds are mounds of clay.
>
> Job 13:12
>
> NRSV translates: Your maxims are proverbs [*mashal* term] of ashes/Your defenses are defenses of clay.

The word *zikārōn* from *zkr*, "to remember," nowhere else means a saying or "maxim" (NRSV) of some sort. If we translate this term in a way truer to its root meaning "memorial," then *gab* in the second line of the bicolon is best translated "mound," the *gab* being most literally a "round thing" (cf. pile of stones in Josh 4:9). Dust and clay are easily dissolved or crumble. What then is "a *mashal* of dust"? The *mashal* appears to be something communicated in a way that is oblique, indirect, abstract, something mirage-like that can dissolve; it is passed down, potentially narrative, something to do with remembrance. Perhaps Job 13:12 suggests that the "memorial" or "remembrance" one leaves behind is only an abstraction, not quite real or concrete, a conceit, something that evokes something else. It is similar to the real thing but not the real thing, a model. Hence the etymological link to "similar to." In Job 13:12, the term *mashal* is used in a quite poetic and therefore ambiguous way, but the notion of *mashal* as stylized "conceit" or "abstraction" or "model" drawing upon memory, an image relevant to a current situation drawn from the proverb-weaver's life, the world of the imagination, or the wider traditions of his/her culture begins to give some hint of the conceptual link between sorts of material placed under the heading *mashal*.

THE HUMAN AS MASHAL

Ezekiel 14:8 provides an interesting use of *mashal* in which Israelites who desert Yahweh for idols are punished, cut off from the people Israel to become a sign (*'ōt*) and a *mashal*. Here and in comparable biblical contexts (Job 17:6; Ps 44:14 [v. 15 in Hebrew]; 69:12; Deut 28:37; 1 Kgs 9:7; 2 Chron 7:20; Jer 24:9 [v. 14 in the English]; Joel 2:17) the term is usually translated "byword" (so Greenberg:246; Eichrodt:179; Zimmerli:302, 308). In trying to place this usage of *mashal* in a recognizable *mashal* category, Zimmerli writes ". . . in the 'byword' the knowledge of this [what had previously been hidden: judgement upon the idolator] comes to the mouths of all people and is hardened into a fixed saying, stuck in every memory like a proverb" (308). Thus he tries to equate *mashal*/proverb/"byword." Polk is more on track when he describes the prophet as a "paradigm," "an archetype of a bad fate" (577; see also Landes:142). And yet Zimmerli's emphasis on memory is helpful. The human *mashal* is an icon or exemplar who becomes a part of the tradition to be stylized, remembered, analogized, and cited. And the meaning of the human *mashal* remains ambiguous and can be variously interpreted depending upon the context in which he is cited.

MASHALS THAT LOOK LIKE PROVERBS

We now turn to places in which brief language indicates that something considered a *mashal* is about to be quoted or created, for example, "All who draw *mashal* (pl.) will draw a *mashal* saying. . . ." A saying, story, or some other literary form then follows the rubric. Ezekiel provides an interesting set of *meshalim*, introduced by *mashal* rubrics.

First comes a category of sayings that sound like proverbs as variously defined by Dundes (1975), Fontaine, Crenshaw (1974:231), and others. Fontaine defines the "traditional saying" as

> a statement, current among the folk, which is concise,
> syntactically complete, consisting of at least one topic
> and comment which may or may not be metaphorical,
> but which exhibits a logical relationship between its
> terms. Further, the saying may be marked by stylistic
> features (mnemonics, rhythm, alliteration, assonance,
> etc.) or be constructed along recognizable frames
> ("Better A than B . . . ," etc.) which distinguish it from
> other genres (or folk idioms). The referents which form
> the image are most likely to be drawn from the experi-
> ence of common, "everyday" life, but the meaning
> (message) of the saying may vary from context to con-
> text, and any "truth claim" for that message must be
> considered "relative" rather than "absolute." The trans-
> mission of the saying, however achieved, is *always* pur-
> poseful, but specific details of contextual use may be
> necessary to determine the purpose in any given situ-
> ation."
>
> Fontaine:64

Ezek 16:44–45 provides a first example. "All who draw *mashal* will draw a *mashal* about you saying 'Like the mother is her daughter.' The daughter of your mother you are, who loaths her husband and her children. . ."

This proverb is what Dundes would call a nonoppositional, multide-scriptive element proverb, comparable to "like father like son." The topic is "daughter," the comment "like the mother" (see Fontaine:244–51). In fact, the gloss on this proverb may be a proverb itself, another equational proverb in the second person: "You are your mother's daughter." The syntactic pattern of the saying in v. 44 is found elsewhere in Scripture (Judg 8:21) while the theme of the saying is found throughout the world. Ezekiel here uses the saying to criticize Israel for her faithlessness to God and invokes the metaphor of the harlot used by him, Hosea, Jeremiah, and other biblical writers. Ezekiel reminds Israel of folk genealogies about its ancient Near Eastern progenitors, all polytheistic idolaters who are un-clean from Ezekiel's perspective. And so, Israel should not be overly proud, for as the Rabbis say one should not say to converts, "Just yester-day, swine's flesh was sticking out from between her teeth."

The folklorist exploring context to understand meaning would be most interested in other instances in which this saying was used in ancient Is-rael. Was the saying ever potentially neutral or positive as is "like father like son" or "he's a chip off the old block" in our culture? Was the generational comparison at the heart of this proverb always a negative one when female imagery was involved and if so why? Again feminist questions intertwine with folkloristic ones. Given that this proverb is used nowhere else in biblical literature, we have to leave these questions unanswered although they are useful questions.

In what way is this *mashal*, a conceit or a model, possibly drawn from memory? Does the etymology rooted in "similar" remain apt? Is this saying *mashal* "metaphoric" (see Dundes 1975; in Mieder and Dundes:52–53)? Israel and the Hittites are not really women; Israel and the Hittites are different neighboring cultural groups. The proverbial saying's context links these two cultures via the metaphor of family. Here, however, we come to the difficult boundary where myth meets metaphor. The tradition has it that Israel *is* "genetically" related to the people around her. On one level, to Ezekiel and his audience, Israel may well be the daughter of a Hittite mother and an Aramaean father. The proverb as glossed thus dips into recognized and accepted tradition, a story about origins that has to do with strong tensions in Israel's own sense of self, her own identity. Does Israel have a unique culture born of Yahwism or is her culture a mere variation on shared ancient Near Eastern themes? While the saying itself, "like mother like daughter," reveals worries about individual identity—Who do we look like or act like? How much are we for better or worse our parents' children?—Ezek 16:44 places this psychological dilemma in larger cultural terms (for proverbs as expressions of social and psychological tensions, see Seitel:132–33).

In telegraphic ways, the saying reveals and encapsulates a particular set of social concerns, providing "models" on various levels. Geertz's language describing religion as a cultural system, offering "models of" and "models for" society, is helpful here (see also Polk's discussion of the "noetic," the "normative," and paradigms [569, 573, 578–79, 583]). This saying offers a genuine model of Israel. She believes herself an ancient Near Eastern people who shares origins with the surrounding nations. And yet given its context in Ezekiel, the saying provides an implicit proscriptive model for society: It is bad to be like "your mother." Change your ways; let nurture (God's influence) rather than nature (foreign genetics) govern who you are. The saying thus finds an appropriate place in Ezekiel's larger story (chap. 16) of the man who finds an abandoned baby weltering in her blood, and cleanses, adopts, and raises her.

This notion of "model of/model for" also appears to fit Ezek 18:2–3, another *mashal* drawing upon a generational theme.

> Why do you [lit. What is it to you to] draw
> this *mashal* about [lit. over] the land of Israel saying
>
> > "The parents eat sour grapes
> > But the teeth of the children are set on edge" ["soured"
> > or "grow blunt like an ax"]?
>
> (See Zimmerli, 378)

The prophet employs the *mashal* to underscore the Deuteronomic theology of the sins of the parents being visited on future generations (Ex 34:7; 20:5; Num 14:18) and to critique it. No longer will this worldview pertain, for each person will be punished for his own sins. It is, in fact, a measure of the radical nature of Ezekiel's message that he cites an apparent piece of tradition, a terse expression or a brief model of Israelite worldview, to deny its future relevance. Thus the "model of reality," a basic tenet of the way of the world, becomes a model for a new reality, the better imagining, the way the world should be. A thread of the old myth is rejected and a new one built upon it.

This *mashal* is an analogy (contrast Herbert:185); the prophet is not speaking of teeth and grapes but drawing a comparison between a stylized cameo about parents eating and children's teeth being affected and a current belief about the sins of parents being visited on the children. And in fact he says the analogy will no longer apply.

Like the saying in Ezek 16:44, this one draws upon a universal concern with relationships between the generations. Does the evil that we do live after us, to borrow Shakespeare's coining of the sentiment in *Julius Caesar*? How much are we our parents' children, affected by what they do? How much are our actions and our fates in our control? Ultimately, how much control do we have? The commentary in Ezekiel's rejection of this saying indicates a particular view about the roots of suffering. Each person should be held responsible for his or her actions and rewarded or punished accordingly. Ideally, suffering should not be the result of the sins of one's parents.

The *mashal*, then, is an expression of worldview, a model of reality, a form of analogic communication that encapsulates essential ideas about the way the world works. Here that particular expression is rejected.

The same definition works for Ezekiel's *mashal* in 12:22–23, where Ezekiel cites and then rejects a saying introduced formulaically with *mashal* language:

> Son of man,
> Why do you draw this *mashal* against [lit. "What is this *mashal*

> to you over"]
> the land of Israel saying,
> "The days are long
> Every vision is ephemeral" [lit. "is lost"].

This saying is usually translated and interpreted to mean that no prophecies come true, even though time runs on: "The days grow long and nothing happens of all the visions" (Zimmerli: 279, 280–81); "Time runs on and every vision comes to nothing" (Greenberg:226–27); "The days grow long and every vision comes to contempt" (Eichrodt:147; see also his discussion on pp. 155–56). This proverb can be read, however, less specifically to contrast reality with pipe dreams: the wearing on of "real time" versus the inevitable quick dissolution of visions, the drudgery and reality of daily life versus the ephemeral nature of dreams. This saying could refer to positive or negative visions depending upon the context. It could be a call to action and self-reliance or a statement about the loss of dreams and hope. Dreams and visions of course need not be good ones. Ezekiel refers to visions of doom and so in his context the proverb becomes a cynical comment on all visions of the future. But as in 18:2–3, Ezekiel rejects the old truth as contextualized in chap. 12 and, in fact, provides an alternate saying mimicking the structure and reversing the content and meaning of the inherited wisdom it echoes.

> Days draw near
> And the matter of every vision.
>
> Ezek 12:23

Time does not drag but hastens as does the fulfillment of visions. The second colon, thereby, is made parallel to the first.

The *mashal* on a basic level is a veritable cosmogonic comment on the nature of the world that points to a tension in human existence between reality and expectations, between the status quo and change. Although the saying is not metaphoric (days do not stand for something else) it does provide a telegraphic, shorthand general statement about the way the world works that can be applied to a specific situation or setting or that can be rejected (see also 1983:573). In this sense it communicates compactly.

INCANTATION/ORACLE/SIGN ACT AS *MASHAL*

Ezek 24:3–13 is not a saying that would fit Fontaine's and others' definitions of proverb. Ezekiel is ordered to deliver a *mashal* to the rebellious house: "Thus says the Lord, Yahweh." The *mashal* is thus God's message, a message in symbols evocative of the sign acts in which biblical prophets are commanded to manipulate objects creating a cameo scene that is then interpreted to hold information about the people's status and future.

In this case, the symbol involves setting up a pot of boiling water filled with choice animal meat and bones. The command to Ezekiel has the rhythmic and alliterative quality of incantation (one thinks of the witches in *MacBeth*). Zimmerli suggests that this is a work song (499). Sign acts not only symbolize events and situations but also through sympathetic magic help to bring them about (see moves in this direction in A. R. Johnson: 167–169, Herbert:182, 195–96; also Niditch, 1980b:34). The "pieces" are interpreted to be the contents of the "bloody city," the pot, Jerusalem itself imagined to be a rusty, filthy container requiring a radical purging. This image of the boiling pot found also in Jer 1:13 where it symbolizes imminent destruction as punishment is here greatly elaborated with attention to themes of ritual preparation and a priestly interest in purity typical of Ezekiel. The "model" aspect of the *mashal* genre is clear in this happening with the pot in which objects are consciously representational, manipulated, and interpreted as symbolic even while helping to bring about what they predict. The pot *mashal* is a model of Israel's status as full of sin and of her future to undergo a refinement as in the imagery of Isa 1:25; 6:13; Ezek 22:20–22; Zech 13:8–9; Mal 3:2–3. The model comes from God in a spoken word that merges with the prophet's imagination and the imagery of his tradition. God thus speaks in oblique speech, veiled images that approach the matter at hand in an allusive and analogical fashion. This serves to emphasize God's mysteriousness and the prophet's participation in the mystery (on Ezek 17 and mystery, see Polk:578). It also says something important about modes of communication between the divine and the human mediated by the prophet and about statuses in those relationships.

Just as the sayings called *mashal* explored above point to tensions between generations, to important questions of identity, and to matters of myth and reality (in Eliade's sense), all pieces of the big question about the human being's place in and experience of the world, so this *mashal* in a form of narrative dramatic action, points to the distance between the divine and the human and the control that God has over humankind. God is not easy to understand; his messages in their indirectness can have infinite and wide-ranging application, as the scholarly debate over the real meaning of this passage illustrates (see Eichrodt:337–39). The message that is not lost in the specifics of this *mashal* is that God is the wizard, the prophet his apprentice, and the rest of the people on some level pieces of meat in a pot. The indirect *mashal* thus puts Israel in her place more completely than any direct word oracle. The expounder of the *mashal* has the power of knowing, the power to put his spin on reality, for the *mashal* is a model. The meaning of the *mashal* of the eagle in Ezekiel 17 is also mysterious, oblique, and God's to control.

The difficulty of interpreting Ezekiel 17 is even greater than problems posed by Ezek 24:3–13, and with this difficulty the emphasis on analogy as mystery is heightened. This tale is not precisely one thing but approaches something; it is evocative, analogous. The power of the weaver of the *mashal* is enhanced, the reader's sense of impotence is increased, the applicability of the scene widened (on this process, see Polk:582–83). Greenberg translates *mashal* here as "fable." Noting the difficulty of understanding the symbolic scenes about eagle, a cedar shoot, a seed, and vines, and of explaining precisely the connection between the symbols and the interpretation, Greenberg asks how Ezekiel's listeners would have decoded his message? (321) Questions about this story of plantings and birds are also asked about symbolic visions such as Daniel 7. Was the story or the vision see-through to its own audience but difficult for us to understand only because our culture and codes differ from those of the Israelites or was the imagery just as strange to the ancient audience? I suggest that a good *mashal*—whether a saying, a symbolic action, or a symbolic story—was designed to be oblique (contrast Landes:145, who suggests that the prophet makes clear how the ambiguous and potentially "inexplicable" *mashal* is meant to be interpreted), testing the listener's capacity to make sense, allowing for various interpretations and levels of meaning; it is indirect communication through analogies. But what is analogous to what? (For some various ways of making sense of Ezekiel 17 in its own sociohistorical context of exile, see the reviews of options by Greenberg:309–24; Eichrodt:223–31; and Zimmerli:354-368.) As Michael D. Lieber has shown (426–27), analogical structures are necessarily "pervasively ambiguous." Is the first eagle Nebuchadnezzar and the second Pharaoh? Is the seed the Israelite king or Israel? What is the good soil? Whatever happened to the cedar shoot? The interpretation provided in Ezekiel is not all that clear. And, in fact, vv. 22–24 offer a quite different reading of the *mashal* than 17:11–21. The biblical pericope in current form thus testifies to the reapplicability and artful ambiguity of the *mashal*.

Greenberg notes that the prophet is directed *hûd hîdāh* (to produce the dark or indirect speech most commonly translated "riddle") and *meshol mashal* (to weave a "fable" or "allegory" are the usual translations). He suggests that Ezekiel 17 operates on two levels, the plane of the riddle which is opaque and mystifying and the plane of the *mashal* or "fable" that draws a more overt comparison. Here, Greenberg notes, the *mashal* is infused with the mystery of *hîdāh* (309) while the *hîdāh* becomes an allegory that shows "all political transactions" to be "but a likening (*mašal*) to the relations between God and the Judahite king" (322–23). *Hîdāh* and *mashal*, however, are frequently used in parallelism (noted also by Polk:578, n. 51; see also Hab 2:6). The *mashal* is never direct and obvious but in some ways always points beyond itself.

A *mashal* rubric implicitly asks if the listener wishes to participate. (Polk:573) That is, the *mashal* can be treated respectfully as a source of self-knowledge and wisdom or as the ravings of a pedant at best, a madman at worse. As our own culture uses the term "myth" variously to mean source of ultimate truth or untrue story, so the weaver of *mashal* can be a wiseman and a prophet or a charlatan; the *mashal* itself can be a model of truth or a byword, to be mocked and discredited, a source of derision. So in Ezek 21:5, the prophet claims that others say of him "Is he not [merely] a weaver of *mashal*'s!" For them the emperor has no clothes. His "models" for them are not compact statements of worldview, of what is or is about to be but just empty mirrors, inventions, abstractions, unreal. In Polk's terms "they [the people] reject the prophet's truth claim" (576).

Before attempting a definition of the Israelite genre *mashal*, one question remains. Have we gained a sense of Ezekiel's use of the term "*mashal*" without developing a definition of an Israelite ethnic genre? Polk, for example, limits his study only to the Book of Ezekiel. One can find good echoes of Ezekiel's usages, however, outside of Ezekiel. The sort of sayings that suit Fontaine's definition of proverb (Ezek 16:44; 18:2–3) are found also in the book of Proverbs and elsewhere (for example 1 Sam 24:14 [13 in English]) as Eissfeldt has shown. The narrative visionary *mashal* in Isa 14 parallels the type of *mashal* found in Ezekiel 17; the "negative model" of Ezekiel finds parallels in Job 17:6; Ps 44:14; Deut 28:37; etc.

MASHAL OUTSIDE OF EZEKIEL

Other biblical discourses not as obviously comparable to the cases in Ezekiel are also introduced by *mashal* terminology: 1 Sam 10:12 and Num

21:27—sayings based on and alluding to larger narrative tradtions; Job 27:1ff. and 29:1ff., a discourse on the lot of the wicked and Job's remembrance of his life before suffering; Hab 2:6ff.—a series of woe oracles; Mic 2:4, a lament of sorts; Num 23:7ff., 24:3ff.,15ff.,20ff.,21ff.,23ff., oracles. Given what we have learned from Ezekiel, how do these qualify as *mashal*?

The saying in 1 Sam 10:12 introduced by *mashal* language—"Is Saul too among the prophets"—is rich in the artful ambiguity discussed by Lieber (see his discussion of this and nonbiblical proverbs). What distinguishes both it and the saying in Num 21:27 is that they are so closely associated with and claimed to be derived from narrative events in the tradition. Saul's behavior is said to give rise to the proverb, while the saying, "Come to Heshbon, let it be built; let the city of Sihon be established," is associated with a supposed encapsuling or remembering of Sihon's successful capture of Moab's land in which his own inheritance was established, an inheritance now conquered by Israel. Num 21:27 is a saying about a story within a story, and it is interesting to ask what the saying is supposed to relate to in the biblical context. Is it now quoted ironically to show how great Sihon's fall is? (See Landes's suggestion [143] that perhaps too woodenly forces this and other cases of *mashal* into a particular notion of *mashal* as "example.") Lieber discusses the interesting ways in which the Saul proverb might have been employed in conversation: as a comment on erratic behavior (see also nuances suggested by Herbert:183); as a statement that someone is "putting on airs"; to say as we do "everyone wants to get into the act" (where perhaps they have no real place); and so on. Sayings about cities that rely on information or traditions about them or characteristics about them are found in our own tradition, for example "Rome wasn't built in a day" or "It's like bringing coals to Newcastle." At the heart of the biblical saying about Heshbon seems to be a model of action in high gear. In any event, the *mashal* is derived from a larger tradition about the establishment of Heshbon by Sihon.

Both of these sayings are directly drawn from stories and are, in effect, shorthand reminders or tag-lines of those stories (see Finnegan, 1970:391). It may be, in fact, that the mention of one of these sayings brought or was meant to bring to the listeners' attention aspects of the larger stories about Saul's prophecying and Sihon's conquests because of their relevance to a current situation. We no longer have a full version of Sihon's story that would help to situate and contextualize the saying *mashal* in the tradition, explaining the meaning the saying and its background story might have held in a live setting. This sort of *mashal* saying points, however, to the importance of tradition, memory, modeling, ambiguity, and compactness in the Israelite concept of *mashal*, traits we have seen in Ezekiel.

Job 27:1 begins as a speech appropriate to the alternating lament and lawsuit forms of the book (27:1–12). In vv. 11–12, however, the *mashal* quality of the discourse, as we have come to understand *mashal*, becomes clear.

> "I will instruct you concerning the hand of God,
> That which is with the Almighty I will not conceal."

Job is about to share an imaging of the ways of God, another of these cameos drawn from experience and observation, filtered through the imagination and stylized—an aspect of the world in miniature. "All of you have seen it yourselves" (v. 12) but "it" needs to be placed in relief by Job to become a model. Job goes on to describe the eventual lot of the wicked with wonderfully extended detail, drawing one into a series of miniscenes as the wicked, now stripped of possessions, are overtaken by terrors, carried off in the whirlwind at night (see also Ps 49:9,10–15,17–20). Job's memory in 29:1ff. of his life before his troubles is a happier cameo. He makes himself into a model of equanimity in describing his everyday actions and especially the way people related to him with respect. In chap. 30 this memory as model is contrasted with the realities of his current suffering, his isolation and utter alienation. Habakkuk's woe oracles of 2:6–20, introduced by *mashal* language, set up cameos or sketches relevant for understanding and portraying a current situation or behavior. Not all woe oracles are *mashal*—in fact no others are so introduced; but *mashal* terminology is easily applied to Habakkuk's little scenes of crime and punishment. So the author/redactor understands them. To translate the verbal form of the root *mšl* as "taunt," the noun as "mocking riddle" in Hab 2:6 misses the "imagine yourself" aspect of the oracles (see A. R. Johnson:166; on reader response and *mashal*, see Polk:565,573,578–79). The lament of Mic 2:4 and the oracles of Balaam in Num 23:7–10; 18–24:3–9;15–19;20;21–22, and 23–24 also sketch images of Israel in effective shorthand strokes and envision Israel's future and those of neighboring nations. If all of these word pictures can be considered *mashal*, is not all prophecy or all Scripture *mšl* on some level? To some extent, the answer may be yes, for *mashal* is a very important thought category in ancient Israel. In calling the above examples *mashal* the Israelite writer acknowledges they are only approximations of what was, is, and will be.

The existence of this category in Israelite literature implies a particular way of thinking about verbal relationships between human beings and between God and people. Speech itself can become a mask rather than an unveiler of thoughts. Spoken and dramatic forms can mean several things at once. "Wisdom" becomes a more mysterious phenomenon and the Israelite *moshel* "the crafter of proverbs" can be seen as more numinous than scholastic, the literary forms under the heading *mashal* deconstructing as we listen.

It is allowing for *mashal* as an ethnic genre that leads one to this larger picture of Israelite worldview and to insights about essentials in its categories of thought and literature.

A DEFINITION OF THE ISRAELITE GENRE *MASHAL*

Drawn from personal memory and experience and built upon the traditions that are claimed by a folk group to be its collective memory, the *mashal* is a form of oblique and artful communication that sets up an analogy between the communication (a saying, an icon, a narrative, a symbolic action, or another form) and the real-life settings of the listeners. The *mashal* provides a model of or a model for reality and points to unresolved tensions and ambivalences in Israelite worldviews. Abstract and compact, in its ambiguity of meaning, the *mashal* allows for varying responses and a wide range of applicability.

CONCLUSION

The study of the ethnic genre *mashal* in many ways relies upon the good close examination of literary artifacts that characterizes the field of biblical studies at its best as it does the field of folklore. Indeed a number of biblical scholars have approached *mashal* synchronically, allowing that Israelites had some sort of genre in mind when using the term for various literary forms from sayings to fuller narratives to oracles, and so on. The definition to which we have been drawn touches upon several of the terms and concepts suggested by earlier studies. In 1954, Herbert described the *mashal* as a "parable" in the sense of a "rapidly drawn picture" . . . "compelling the reader to form a judgment on himself, his situation. . . ." The term "model" is found in McKane's 1970 study, and Landes's 1978 study describes *mashal* most essentially as "example." McKane oversimplifies in his use of "model" and Landes too woodenly tries to show how every *mashal* operates as an example of some sort, while Herbert tends to overtheologize the genre. More sophisticated is Polk's article that deals with notions of "model of" and "model for" in the style of Clifford Geertz (although Geertz is not Polk's specific inspiration) and that emphasizes participatory and other important contextual aspects of the *mashal*.

What a folkloristic perspective most adds to our study is a sociolinguistic interest in the ways a verbal and literary genre reflects the culture in which it holds meaning. We are thus interested not only in how Israelites defined and understood *mashal*, but in what this understanding and the very existence of the category reveals about Israelite modes of thought, about Israelite aesthetics and poetics, about attitudes to a host of important and defining cultural issues including attitudes to history, memory, and tradition. It is the interest in the connections between ethnic genre and thoughtworld that distinguishes this folkloristic approach.

Conclusions

Eve's story in Genesis 3, the Passover ritual described in Exodus 12, and the biblical *mashal* pose different sorts of challenges to the biblical folklorist and beckon the application of various combinations of the methodologies reviewed and explored in chapter 1. In each case, biblical folkloristics of some variety has shed new light on some of the well-travelled avenues in the Hebrew Bible.

To study Genesis 3, we gathered together comparable tales about the coming to be of ordinary life on earth and found the cosmological pattern, the morphology, shared by Genesis 3 and tales from other cultures. We asked why such a narrative pattern is important in so many cultures, and about the implications of its central themes for understanding Genesis 3. Then we took note of a more content-specific pattern shared by biblical versions of the morphology, the typology found in Gen 3, 6:1–4, and 11:1–11, and asked what was special about the Israelite version of this story, what the Israelite versions might reveal about a particular cultural tradition and its recurring concerns. Finally, we looked closely at this one particular Israelite telling, exploring issues of author and audience.

The study of Genesis 3 is also informed by the psychoanalytical interests of folklore, by the observations of cultural anthropologists Turner and Lévi-Strauss about cosmogonies, rites of passage, and tricksters, and by the interests of folklore and women's studies. The latter helps one to reach an understanding of the portrayal of Eve, her function in the story and the implications of her role for later appropriations. Freed from Augustine, Milton, and a hoary history of androcentric, normatively grounded interpretations of Genesis 3, we found a tale presenting humans as curious seekers of knowledge, birthed by a woman, coaxed by a trickster. The Israelite author views human beings as inevitably bound to an uneven relationship with God, the parent, and to reality with its good and bad aspects and its cycles of birth, life work, and death.

Chapter 3 continued the study of patterning, exploring the constellations of creation motifs found in the first half of the book of Exodus. Focussing in on Exodus 12, we explored the patterns of symbols in the account of the Passover again with assistance from the methodological approaches of Turner and Lévi-Strauss. This study of a ritual narrative reveals a worldview that strongly demarcates between Israel and the outside world and that treats all Israelites as a community of equals who partake of God's food while effecting a passage from one status to another. Close analysis of symbols of lamb, blood, bitter herbs, and unleavened bread and the mode of preparation and consumption in Exodus 12, calls into question old assumptions about the priestly origins of this passage and leads, in turn, to a comparison with other biblical descriptions of the Passover ritual. Deuteronomy and traditions in 2 Chronicles portray Passover celebrations that are more in tune than is Exodus 12 with certain normative and more usual biblical assumptions about Israelite religion and social structure. Attention to the multilayered meanings of symbols in the Passover ritual thus uncovers the radical quality of one version of an important thread in Israel's foundation mythology and becomes an innovative means of doing tradition history.

Chapter 4 reviewed biblical work on the proverb influenced by folklore studies, and then with help from the studies of Ben-Amos and Finnegan we explored the *mashal* as an "ethnic genre," asking what Israelite authors and audiences meant when they used or heard the term. What does the existence of this category of literature reveal about Israelite modes of communication and verbal confrontation, about the ways in which Israelites made sense of the memory and experiences of individuals and the group, applying them in compact form to comprehend and categorize new situations? The *mashal* as an ethnic genre also speaks to the issue of Israelite attitudes to its own sacred literature.

Certain folkloristic interests have informed all our studies: the interest in comparative literary and ethnographic materials from other cultures; the tracking of cross-culturally recurring pieces and patterns of content and questions about essential human concerns and modes of thought reflected in Israelite literature; close attention to the unique qualities of the Israelite texts; the attempt to understand content and patterns of content in narrative, ritual, and "wisdom" genres and the special culturally or temporally or individually bound messages these convey; the related interest in the life settings of biblical texts that are not to be treated as dead words on bound pages but as the artistic, living creations of human beings who find their place at some special locus in a lengthy biblical tradition. What do the texts communicate and to whom? Who were their intended audiences? How do these texts illuminate the central concerns and interests of individual Israelites, of larger Israelite folk groups in particular socio-historical settings? Do the texts touch upon recurring themes (such as the relationship between God and Israel) relevant to Israelite religion of any period? Even more widely, do they touch upon problems at the core of humanity—questions of gender, questions about attitudes to authority, questions about life and death.

To introduce folklore and the Bible is a much more complicated task than explaining text criticism or form criticism, as have other excellent books in this series, for folklore is an interdiscipline, variously defined and applied. It is a particularly important cross-discipline for contemporary biblical scholarship that sometimes seems to be bifurcated between those who do "new literary studies" and those who do the more traditional study of the history and literature of Israel. Folklorists insist upon the importance of treating pieces of lore as valuable artistic wholes worthy of study in and of themselves, but also seek to understand lore in context, in terms of the authors and audiences for whom texts are meaningful. As such, folklore is a means of enhancing the appreciation and understanding of biblical texts in and of themselves and an added tool in explaining the intellectual and cultural history of the people Israel and the way these relate to the complex threads of biblical tradition.

Bibliography

Aarne, Antti
  1910   *Verzeichnis der Märchentypen*. FFC3. Helsinki: Suomalainen tiedeakatemia.

Abrahams, Roger D.
  1968   "Introductory Remarks to a Rhetorical Theory Folklore." *JAF* 81:143–58.
  1972a   "Personal Power and Social Restraint in the Definition of Folklore." In *Toward New Perspectives in Folklore*, ed. Américo Paredes and Richard Bauman, 16–30.
  1972b   "Proverbs and Proverbial Expressions." In *Folklore and Folklife*, ed. Richard M. Dorson, 117–27. Chicago: University of Chicago Press.

Alter, Robert
  1990   "Samson Without Folklore." In *Text and Tradition: The Hebrew Bible and Folklore*, 47–56. Semeia Studies, ed. Susan Niditch. Atlanta: Scholars Press.

Baldwin, Karen
  1985   "'Woof!' A Word on Women's Roles in Family Storytelling." In *Women's Folklore, Women's Culture*, ed. Jordan and Kalčik, 149–62.

Bauman, Richard
  1986a   *Story, Performance and Event*. Cambridge Studies in Oral and Literater Culture 10. Cambridge: Cambridge University Press.
  1986b   "Performance and Honor in 13th Century Iceland." *JAF* 99:131–50.

Bauman, Richard and Joel Sherzer, eds.
  1974   *Explorations in the Ethnography of Speaking*. Cambridge: Cambridge University Press.

Ben-Amos, Dan
  1966   "Narrative Forms in the Haggadah: Structural Analysis." Ph.D. Diss. Bloomington: Indiana University Press.

1972   "Toward a Definition of Folklore in Context." In *Toward New Perspectives in Folklore*, ed. A. Paredes and R. Bauman, 3–15.

1976a   "Analytical Categories and Ethnic Genres." In *Folklore Genres*, ed. Dan Ben-Amos.

1990   "Comments on Robert C. Culley's 'Five Tales of Punishment in the Book of Numbers.'" In *Text and Tradition*, ed. Susan Niditch, 35–45.

1992a   "Historical Poetics and Generic Shift: *Nifla'ot Ve-Nissim*." (Hebrew) *Jerusalem Studies in Jewish Folklore* 13/14:29–59. Essays in Honor of Dov Noy. Jerusalem: Hebrew University Press.

1992b   "Do We Need Ideal Types (in Folklore)? An Address to Lauri Honko." In *NIF* (Nordic Institute of Folklore) *Papers*: 3–35. Turku, Finland: Nordic Institute of Folklore.

Ben-Amos, Dan, ed.

1976b   *Folklore Genres*. Publication of the American Folklore Society, Bibliographical and Special Series 26. Austin: University of Texas Press.

Ben-Amos, Dan and Kenneth S. Goldstein, eds.

1975   *Folklore: Performance and Communication*. The Hague and Paris: Mouton.

Bottigheimer, Ruth B.

1987   *Grimms' Bad Girls and Bold Boys: The Moral and Social Vision of the Tales*. New Haven: Yale University Press.

1991   "From Gold to Guilt: The Forces Which Reshaped *Grimms' Tales*." In *The Brothers Grimm and Folktale*, ed. James M. McGlathery, 192–204.

Brown, Francis, S. R. Driver, and Charles A. Briggs (BDB)

1968   *A Hebrew and English Lexicon of the Old Testament*. Oxford: Clarendon Press, 1907.

Bynum, David E.

1976   "The Generic Nature of Oral Epic Poetry." *Folklore Genres*, ed. Dan Ben-Amos, 35–58. Austin: University of Texas Press.

1978   *The Daemon in the Wood. A Study of Oral Narrative Patterns*. Cambridge, MA: Center for the Study of Oral Literature.

1980   "Myth and Ritual: Two Faces of Tradition." In *Oral Tradional Literature*, ed. John Miles Foley, 142–63.

1990   "Samson as a Biblical φὴρ ὀρεσκῷος." In *Text and Tradition*, ed. Susan Niditch, 57–73.

Camp, Claudia V.
1985   *Wisdom and the Feminine in the Book of Proverbs.*
                Bible and Literature 2. Sheffield: Almond.
1990   "The Female Sage in Ancient Israel and in the Biblical
                Wisdom Literature." In *The Sage in Israel and the An-
                cient Near East,* ed. John G. Gammine and Leo G.
                Purdue, 185–203. Winona Lake: Eisenbrauns.
Campbell, Joseph
1949   *The Hero with a Thousand Faces.* Bollingen Series 17.
                Princeton: Princeton University Press.
Childs, Brevard S.
1974   *The Book of Exodus. A Critical Theological Commen-
                tary.* Philadelphia: Westminster.
Coote, Robert P.
1976a   "Tradition, Oral, OT." *The Interpreter's Dictionary of
                the Bible, Supplementary Volume,* ed. Keith Crim, 914–
                16. Nashville: Abingdon.
1976b   "The Application of the Oral Theory to Biblical Hebrew
                Literature." *Semeia* 5:51–64.
Creed, Robert P.
1986   "The Remaking of *Beowulf.*" In *Oral Tradition in Liter-
                ature,* ed. John Miles Foley, 136–46.
Crenshaw, James L.
1974   "Wisdom." In *Old Testament Form Criticism,* ed. John
                H. Hayes, 225–64. San Antonio: Trinity University
                Press.
1976   "Studies in Ancient Israelite Wisdom: Prolegomenon."
                In *Studies in Ancient Israelite Wisdom,* ed. James L.
                Crenshaw, 1–45.
Crenshaw, James L. ed.
1976   *Studies in Ancient Israelite Wisdom.* New York: KTAV.
Culley, Robert C.
1963   "An Approach to the Problem of Oral Tradition." *VT*
                13:113–25.
1967   *Oral Formulaic Language in the Biblical Psalms.* Near
                and Middle East Series 4. Toronto: University of To-
                ronto Press.
1972   "Oral Tradition and Historicity." In *Studies on the
                Ancient Palestinian World,* ed. J. W. Wevers and
                D. B. Redford, 102–16. Toronto: University of Toronto
                Press.
1976a   *Studies in the Structure of Hebrew Narrative.* Semeia
                Supplements 3. Missoula: Scholars Press.
1976b   "Oral Tradition and the OT: Some Recent Discussion."
                Semeia 5:1–33.

1986   "Oral Tradition and Biblical Studies." *Oral Tradition*
               1:30–65.
1990   "Five Tales of Punishment in the Book of Numbers." In
               Text and Tradition, ed. Susan Niditch, 25–34.
Culley, Robert C. and Thomas W. Overholt
1982   *Anthropological Perspectives on Old Testament Proph-
               ecy.* Semeia 21. Chico: Scholars Press.
de Vaux, Roland
1961   *Ancient Israel. Its Life and Institutions.* New York:
               McGraw-Hill.
Darr, Kathe Pfisterer
forthcoming   "No Strength to Deliver: A Contextual Reading of Hez-
               ekiah's Proverb in Isa 37:3b." In *Isaiah's Vision and the
               Family of God*, chap. 6.
Detienne, Marcel
1977   *Dionysos mis à mort.* Paris: Gallinard.
1977b   *The Gardens of Adonis: Spices in Greek Mythology,*
               Trans. J. Lloyd. Atlantic Highlands, NJ: Humanities.
Dorson, Richard
1972   *Folklore: Selected Essays.* Bloomington: Indiana Uni-
               versity Press.
Douglas, Mary
1966   *Purity and Danger.* New York: Praeger.
Dundes, Alan
1965a   *The Morphology of North American Indian Tales.* FFC
               195. Helsinki. Suomalainen tiedeakatemia.
1965b   "Structural Typology in North American Indian Folk-
               tales." In *The Study of Folklore*, ed. Alan Dundes,
               206–15.
1971   "The Making and Breaking of a Friendship as a Struc-
               tural Frame in African Folk Tales." In *Structural Analy-
               sis of Oral Tradition*, ed. Pierre Maranda and Elli Kön-
               gäs Maranda, 171–85. Philadelphia: University of
               Pennsylvania Press.
1975   "On the Structure of the Proverb." *Proverbium* 25:961–
               73. (Reprinted in Mieder and Dundes, 1981).
1980   "The Hero Pattern and the Life of Jesus." In *Interpre-
               ting Folklore*, 231–61. Bloomington: Indiana Univer-
               sity Press.
1988   "Interpreting 'Little Red Riding Hood' Psychoanalyti-
               cally." In *The Brothers Grimm and Folktale*, ed. James
               M. McGlathery, 16–51.
Dundes, Alan, ed.
1965c   *The Study of Folklore.* Englewood Cliffs, NJ: Prentice-
               Hall.

1982	*Cinderella: A Folklore Casebook.* New York: Garland.
1989	*Little Red Riding Hood: A Casebook.* Madison, WI: University of Wisconsin Press.

Eliade, Mircea
1954	*The Myth of the Eternal Return: or, Cosmos and History.* Bollingen Series 46. Princeton, NJ: Princeton University Press.

Eichrodt, Walther
1970	*Ezekiel: A Commentary.* Philadelphia: Westminster.

Eissfeldt, Otto
1913	*Der Maschal im Alten Testament.* Beihefte zur ZAW. Giessen: Töpelmann.

Ellis, John
1983	*One Fairy Story too Many: The Brothers Grimm and Their Tales.* Chicago: University of Chicago Press.

Fewell, Danna N. and David M. Gunn
1990	*Compromising Redemption: Relating Characters in the Book of Ruth.* Louisville: Westminster/John Knox.

Finnegan, Ruth
1970	*Oral Literature in Africa.* Oxford: Clarendon.
1973	"Literacy Versus Non-Literacy: The Great Divide?" In *Modes of Thought,* ed. Robin Horton and Ruth Finnegan, 112–44. London: Faber and Faber.
1974	"How Oral is Oral Literature?" *Bulletin of the School of Oriental and African Studies* 37:52–64.
1977	*Oral Poetry: Its Nature, Significance, and Social Context.* Cambridge: Cambridge University Press.
1982	"Oral Literature and Writing in the South Pacific." In *Oral and Traditional Literatures,* ed. Norman Simms, 22–36.
1988	*Literacy and Orality.* Oxford: Basil Blackwell.

Foley, John Miles
1980b	"The Oral Theory in Context." In *Oral Traditional Literature,* ed. John Miles Foley, 27–122.
1988	*The Theory of Oral Composition: History and Methodology.* Bloomington: Indiana University Press.
1992	"Word-Power, Performance, and Tradition." *JAF* 105:275–301.

Foley, John Miles, ed.
1980a	*Comparative Research on Oral Traditions: A Memorial for Milman Parry.* Columbus: Slavica.
1980b	*Oral Traditional Literature.* A Festschrift for Albert Bates Lord. Columbus: Slavica.
1986	*Oral Tradition in Literature. Interpretation in Context.* Columbia: University of Missouri Press.

Fontaine, Carole R.
1982   *Traditional Sayings in the Old Testament: A Contextual
                Study.* The Bible and Literature 5. Sheffield: Almond.
Fontaine, Carole R. and Claudia V. Camp
1990   "The Words of the Wise and their Riddles." In *Text and
                Tradition*, ed. Susan Niditch, 127–51.
Frazer, James George
1911–1915   *The Golden Bough.* 3rd ed. 12 Vols. London: Mac-
                millan.
Freud, Sigmund
1905   *Der Witz und seine Beziehung zum Unbewussten.*
                Wien: Deuticke.
1913   "Märchenstoffe in Träumen." *Internationale Zeitschrift
                für ärztliche Psychoanalyse* 1:145–51.
Fromm, Erich
1951   *The Forgotten Language: An Introduction to the Un-
                derstanding of Dreams, Fairy Tales and Myths.* New
                York: Rinehart.
Gammie, John G. Walter, A. Brueggemann, W. Lee Humphreys,
and James M. Ward, eds.
1978   *Israelite Wisdom: Theological and Literary Essays
                in Honor of Samuel Terrien.* Missoula, MT: Scholars
                Press.
Gaster, Theodor H.
1949/1962   *Passover: Its History and Traditions.* Boston: Beacon
                (originally published in 1949).
1981   *Myth, Legend, and Custom in the Old Testament.* A
                comparative study with chapters from Sir James G. Fra-
                zer's *Folklore in the Old Testament.* 2 Vols. Gloucester,
                MA: Peter Smith.
Geertz, Clifford
1973   "Religion as a Cultural System." In *The Interpretation
                of Cultures*, 87–125. New York: Basic Books.
Gelber, Lisa B.
1989   "The Development of the Passover Observance: How
                Narrative Shapes the Ritual." Senior Thesis, Amherst
                College, Amherst, MA.
Georges, Robert A. and Alan Dundes
1963   "Toward a Structural Definition of the Riddle." *JAF*
                76:111.
Ginzberg, Louis
1909–1938   *Legends of the Jews.* 7 Vols. Philadelphia: Jewish Publi-
                cation Society of America.
Gitay, Yehoshua
1980   "Deutero-Isaiah: Oral or Written?" *JBL* 99:185–97.

Goody, Jack
1977   *The Domestication of the Savage Mind.* Cambridge: Cambridge University Press.
1987   *The Interface between the Written and the Oral.* Cambridge: Cambridge University Press.
Goody, Jack, ed.
1968   *Literacy in Traditional Societies.* Cambridge: Cambridge University Press.
Gordis, Robert
1939/40   "Quotations in Wisdom Literature." *JQR* 30:123–147, (reprinted in Crenshaw, 1976:220–44).
Graham, William A.
1987   *Beyond the Written Word: Oral Aspects of Scriptures in the History of Religion.* Cambridge: Cambridge University Press.
Greenberg, Moshe
1983   *Ezekiel 1–20.* Anchor Bible 22. Garden City: Doubleday.
Greimas, Algirdas Julien
1965   "Le Conte populaire russe (analyse fonctionelle)." *International Journal of Linguistics and Poetics* 9:152–75.
1966   *Sémantique.* Paris: Lacourse.
Gunkel, Hermann
1966   *The Legends of Genesis.* New York: Schocken.
1987   *The Folktale in the Old Testament*, trans. Michael D. Rutter. Sheffield: Almond. Originally published in 1917 as *Das Märchen im Alten Testament.* Tübingen: J. C. B. Mohr.
1910   *Legends of Genesis.* New York: Schocken.
1990   *Genesis.* Göttingen: Vandenhoeck and Ruprecht.
Gunn, David
1974a   "Narrative Patterns and Oral Tradition in Judges and Samuel." *VT* 24:286–317.
1974b   "The 'Battle Report': Oral or Scribal Convention?" *JBL* 93:513–18.
1976   "On Oral Tradition: A Response to John Van Seters." *Semeia* 5:155–61.
1978   *The Story of King David: Genre and Interpretation.* JSOT Supplement Series 6. Sheffield: JSOT.
Hahn, J. G. von
1876   *Sagwissenschaftliche Studien.* Jena: Friedrich Mauke.
Hasan-Rokem, Galit
1982   *Proverbs in Israeli Folk Narratives: A Structural Semantic Analysis.* FFC 232. Helsinki: Finnish Academy of Sciences.

1990   "And God Created the Proverb . . . Inter-Generic and Inter-Textual Aspects of Biblical Paremiology—or the Longest Way to the Shortest Text." In *Text and Tradition*, ed. Susan Niditch, 107–20.

Hendel, Ronald S.
1987   *The Epic of the Patriarch. The Jacob Cycle and the Narrative Traditions of Canaan and Israel*. HSM 42. Atlanta: Scholars Press.

Herbert, A. S.
1954   "The 'Parable' (MAŠAL) in the Old Testament." *Scottish Journal of Theology* 7:180:96.

Holbek, Bengt
1970   "Proverb Style." *Proverbium* 15:470–72.
1987   *Interpretation of Fairy Tales. Danish Folklore in a European Context*. FF Communications 239. Helsinki: Suomalainen Tiedeakatemia.

Hyatt, J. Philip
1971   *Commentary on Exodus*. London: Marshall, Morgan, and Scott.

Hymes, Dell
1974a   "Way of Speaking." In *Explorations in the Ethnography of Speaking*, ed. Richard Bauman and Joel Sherzer, 433–51. Cambridge: Cambridge University Press.
19974b   *Foundations in Sociolinguistics. An Ethnographic Approach*. Philadelphia: University of Pennsylvania Press.
1981   "Breakthrough into Performance." In *"In Vain I Tried to Tell You": Essays in Native American Ethnopoetics*, 79–141. Philadelphia: University of Pennsylvania Press.
1985   "Language, Memory, and Selective Performance: *Cultee's 'Salmon's Myth' as Twice Told to Boas*." *JAF* 98:391–434.

Irvin, Dorothy
1977   "The Joseph and Moses Stories as Narrative in the Light of Ancient Near Eastern Narrative." In *Israelite and Judaean History*, ed. John H. Hayes and J. Maxwell Miller, 180–209. Philadelphia: Westminster.
1978   *Mytharion: The Comparison of Tales from the Old Testament and the Ancient Near East*. Alter Orient und Altes Testament 32. Kevelaer: Butzon & Berker.

Jason, Heda
1971a   "The Narrative Structure of Swindler Tales." *Journal of Scandinavian Folklore* 27:141–60.

1971b	"Proverbs in Society: The Problem of Meaning and Function." *Proverbium* 17:617–23.
1979	"The Story of David and Goliath: A Folk Epic?" *Biblica*, 60:36–70.
1981	"Ilja of Murom and Tzar Kalin: A Proposal for a Model for the Narrative Structure of an Epic Struggle." In *Salvica Hierosolymitana*. Slavic Studies of the Hebrew University, Vols. v-vi, ed. L. Fleishman, O. Ronen, and D. Segal, 47–55. Jerusalem: Magnes Press.
1984	"The Fairytale of the Active Heroine: An Outline for Discussion." In *Le conte, pourquoi, comment?* ed. G. Galame-Griaule, V. Görög-Karady, and M. Chiche, 79–97. Paris: Centre National de la Recerche scientifique.

Jay, Nancy
| 1992 | *Throughout Your Generations Forever: Sacrifice, Religion, and Paternity.* Chicago: University of Chicago Press. |

Johnson, A. R.
| 1955 | "*Māšāl.*" In *Wisdom in Israel and in the Ancient Near East*, ed. M. Noth and D. Winton Thoms. Supplements to *VT* 3, 162–69. Leiden: Brill. |

Jordan, Rosan A. and Susan K. Kalčik
| 1985 | *Women's Folklore, Women's Culture.* Philadelphia: University of Pennsylvania Press. |

Jolles, André
| 1929 | *Einfache Formen.* Halle: Niemeyer. |

Jung, Carl Gustav
| 1948 | "Zur Phänomenologie des Geistes im Märchen." In *Gesammelte Werke* 9/1 (1976), 221–69. |

Kelber, Werner
| 1979 | "Mark and Oral Tradition." *Semeia* 16:7–55="Markus und die mündliche Tradition." *Linguistica Biblica* 45:5–58. |
| 1983 | *The Oral and the Written Gospel.* Philadelphia: Fortress. |

Kirkpatrick, Patricia G.
| 1988 | *The Old Testament and Folklore Study.* JSOT Supplement series 62. Sheffield: JSOT. |

Kirshenblatt-Gimblett, Barbara
| 1973 | "Toward a Theory of Proverb Meaning." *Proverbium* 22:821–27 Reprinted in *The Wisdom of Many*, ed. Mieder and Dundes, 1981:111–21. |
| 1974 | "The Concept and Varieties of Narrative Performance in East European Jewish Culture." In *Explorations in* |

the Ethnography of Speaking, ed. Richard Bauman and Joel Sherzer, 283–308.

Landes, George M.
1978   "Jonah: A Māšsāl?" In Israelite Wisdom, ed. J. G. Gammie et al, 137–58. Missoula: Scholars Press.

Leach, Edmond
1969   Genesis as Myth and Other Essays. London: Jonathan Cape.

Lévi-Strauss, Claude
1968   "The Structural Study of Myth." In Myth: A Symposium, ed. Thomas A. Sebeok, 81–106. Bloomington: Indiana University Press.
1969   The Raw and the Cooked, trans. John and Doreen Weightman. New York: Harper and Row.
1970   Structural Anthropology. New York: Harper and Row.
1978   The Origin of Table Manners. Trans. John and Doreen Weightman. New York: Harper and Row.

Lieber, Michael D.
1984   "Analogic Ambiguity: A Paradox of Proverb Usage." JAF 97:423–41.

Long, Burke O.
1976a   "Recent Field Studies in Oral Literature and the Question of Sitz im Leben." Semeia 5:35–49.
1976b   "Recent Field Studies in Oral Literature." VT 26:187–98.
1982   "The Social Function of Conflict among the Prophets." In Anthropological Perspectives on Old Testament Prophecy, ed. Robert C. Culley and Thomas Overholt, 31–53.

Lord, Albert B.
1968   The Singer of Tales. New York: Atheneum.
1980   "Memory, Fixity and Genre in Oral Traditional Poetries." In Oral Traditional Literature, ed. John Miles Foley, 451–561.
1986   "The Merging of Two Worlds: Oral and Written Poetry as Carriers of Ancient Values." In Oral Tradition in Literature, ed. John Miles Foley, 19–64.
1987   "Characteristics of Orality." Oral Tradition 2. A Festschrift for Walter J. Ong, 54–72. Columbus: Slavica.

Maranda, Elli-Kaija Köngäs
1963   "The Concept of Folklore." Midwest Folklore 13:69–88.

Maranda, Elli Köngäs and Pierre Maranda
1971   Structural Models in Folklore and Transformational Essays. Approaches to Semiotics 10. The Hague and Paris: Mouton.

McKane, William
1970   "The Meaning of *Mašal*." In *Proverbs: A New Ap-proach*, 22–33. London: SCM.

McGlathery, James M., ed.
1988   *The Brothers Grimm and Folktale*. Urbana: University of Illinois Press.

Messenger, John C. Jr.
1959   "The Role of Proverbs in a Nigerian Judicial System." Reprinted in *The Study of Folklore*, ed. Alan Dundes 299–307.

Meyers, Carol
1988   *Discovering Eve: Ancient Israelite Women in Context*. New York and Oxford: Oxford University Press.

Middleton, John
1990   "Comments on Robert Wilson." In *Text and Tradition*, ed. Susan Niditch, 207–13.

Mieder, Wolfgang
1974   "The Essence of Literary Proverb Study." *Proverbium* 23:888–94.

1987   *Tradition and Innovation in Folk Literature*. Hanover, NH: The University Press of New England.

1986   *The Prentice-Hall Encyclopedia of World Proverbs: A Treasury of Wit and Wisdom Through the Ages*. Englewood Cliffs, NJ: Prentice Hall.

Mieder, Wolfgang and Alan Dundes, eds.
1981   *The Wisdom of Many: Essays on the Proverb*. New York: Garland.

Mills, Margaret
1982   "A Cinderella Variant in the Context of a Muslim Women's Ritual." In *Cinderella: A Folklore Casebook*, ed. Alan Dundes, 180–92.

Milne, Pamela J.
1986   "Folktales and Fairy Tales: An Evaluation of Two Proppian Analyses of Biblical Narrative." *JSOT* 34:35–60.

1988   *Vladimir Propp and the Study of Structure in Hebrew Biblical Narrative*. Sheffield: Almond.

Mitchell, Carol
1985   "Some Differences in Male and Female Joke-Telling." In *Women's Folklore, Women's Culture*, ed. R. A. Jordan and S. J. Kalčik, 163–186.

Mowry, L.
1962   "Parable," *IDB* 3:649–54.

Murphy, Roland E.
1981   *Wisdom Literature: Job, Proverbs, Ruth, Canticles, Ec-
               clesiastes and Esther.* Forms of the Old Testament Lit-
               erature 13. Grand Rapids: Eerdmans.
Neumann, Erich
1972   *The Great Mother: An Analysis of the Archetype.*
               Bollingen Series 47. Princeton: Princeton University
               Press.
Niditch, Susan
1980a   "The Composition of Isaiah 1." *Biblica* 61:509–29.
1980b   *The Symbolic Vision in Biblical Tradition.* HSM 30.
               Chico, CA: Scholars Press.
1986   "Ezekiel 40–48 in a Visionary Context." *CBQ*
               48:208–24.
1987   *Underdogs and Tricksters: A Prelude to Biblical Folk-
               lore.* San Francisco: Harper and Row.
1990   "Samson as Culture Hero, Trickster, and Bandit: The
               Empowerment of the Weak." *CBQ* 52:608–24.
1993   *War in the Hebrew Bible: A Study in the Ethics of
               Violence.* New York and Oxford: Oxford University
               Press.
Niditch, Susan and Robert Doran
1977   "The Success Story of the Wise Courtier." *JBL*
               96:179–93.
Niditch, Susan, ed.
1990   *Text and Tradition: The Hebrew Bible and Folklore.*
               Atlanta: Scholars Press.
Noth, Martin
1962   *Exodus: A Commentary.* Philadelphia: Westminster
               (originally published in German in 1959).
Oden, Robert
1981   "Transformations in Near Eastern Myths." *Religion*
               11:21–37.
Olrik, Axel
1909   "Epic Laws of Folk Narrative." In *The Study of Folk-
               lore,* ed. Alan Dundes, 129–41.
Ong, Walter J., S. J.
1982a   "Literacy and Orality in Our Times." In *Oral and Tradi-
               tional Literatures,* ed. Norman Simms, 8–21.
1982b   *Orality and Literacy: The Technologizing of the Word.*
               London: Methuen.
1986   "Text as Interpretation: Mark and After." In *Oral Tradi-
               tion in Literature,* ed. John Miles Foley, 147–69.

Overholt, Thomas
 1986   *Prophecy in Cross-Cultural Perspective: A Sourcebook
                for Biblical Researchers*. Sources for Biblical Study 17.
                Atlanta: Scholars Press.
Paredes, Americo and Richard Baumen
 1972   *Toward New Perspectives in Folklore*. Austin: Univer-
                sity of Texas Press.
Patte, Daniel, ed.
 1960   *Genesis 2 and 3: Kaleidoscopic Structural Readings*.
                Semeia 18.
Pendergast, David M.
 1988   "The Historical Content of Oral Tradition: A Case from
                Belize." *JAF* 101:321–24.
Polk, Timothy
 1983   "Paradigms, Parables, and *Měšālîm*: On Reading *Māšāl*
                in Scripture" *CBQ* 45:564–83.
Polzin, Robert
 1977   *Biblical Structuralism: Method and Subjectivity in the
                Study of Ancient Texts*. Missoula, MT: Scholars Press.
Propp, Vladimir
 1960   *The Morphology of the Folktale*. Austin: University of
                Texas Press.
 1984   *Theory and History of Folktales*, trans. A. Martin and
                R. Martin, ed. A. Liberman. Theory and History of
                Literature 5. Minneapolis: University of Minnesota
                Press.
Rad, Gerhard von
 1961   *Genesis: A Commentary*. Philadelphia: Westminster
                (originally published in German in 1956).
Rank, Otto
 1964   "The Myth of the Birth of the Hero." In *Myth of the
                Birth of the Hero and Other Writings by Otto Rank*, ed.
                Philip Freund. New York: Vintage.
Renoir, Alain
 1986   "Oral Formulaic Rhetoric and the Interpretation of Lit-
                erary Texts." In *Oral Tradition in Literature*, ed. John
                Miles Foley, 103–35.
Ringgren, Helmer
 1949   "Oral and Written Transmission in the O. T.: Some Ob-
                servations." *Studia Theologica*, 3:34–59.
Róheim, Géza
 1989   "Fairy Tale and Dream: 'Little Red Riding Hood'." In
                Little Red Riding Hood: A Casebook, ed. Alan Dundes,
                159–67, (originally published in 1953).

Röhrich, Lutz
1988   "The Quest for Meaning in Folk Narrative Research." In *The Brothers Grimm and Folktales*, ed. James McGlathery, 1–15.

Rölleke, Heinz
1986   "Die Kinder-und Hausmärchen der Brüder Grimm in neuer Sicht." *Diskussion Deutsch* 91:458–64.

1988   "New Results of Research on *Grimms' Fairy Tales*." In *The Brothers Grimm and Folktales*, ed. James McGlathery, 101–11.

Rosenberg, Bruce A.
1987   "The Complexity of Oral Tradition." *Oral Tradition* 2:73–90.

Rowe, Karen E.
1986   "Feminism and Fairy Tales." In *Don't Bet on the Prince*, ed. Jack Zipes, 209–26.

Sarna, Nahum M.
1986   *Exploring Exodus*. New York: Schocken.

Sasson, J. M.
1979   *Ruth: A Translation with a Philological Formalist-Folklorist Interpretation*. Baltimore: Johns Hopkins University Press.

Scott, Charles T.
1976   "On Defining the Riddle: The Problem of a Structural Unit." In *Folklore Genres*, ed. Dan Ben-Amos, 77–90.

Seitel, Peter
1976   "Proverbs: A Social Use of Metaphor." In *Folklore Genres*, ed. Dan Ben-Amos, 125–43, (originally published in 1969 in *Genre* 2:143–161).

Shils, Edward
1981   *Tradition*. Chicago: University of Chicago Press.

Simms, Norman
1982   *Oral and Traditional Literatures. Pacific Quarterly Moana*. 7:2. Hamilton, New Zealand: Outrigger Publishers.

Soll, W. S.
1989   "Misfortune and Exile in Tobit: The Juncture of a Fairy Tale Source and Deuteronomic Theology." *CBQ* 51:209–31.

Speiser, E. A.
1964   *Genesis*. Anchor Bible 1. Garden City: Doubleday.

Street, Brian
1984   *Literacy in Theory and Practice*. Cambridge: Cambridge University Press.

Suter, David
1981   "*Māšāl* in the Similitudes of Enoch." *JBL* 100:193–212.
Sydow, Carl Wilhelm von
1984   "Popular Prose Traditions and Their Classification." In
                Selected Papers on Folklore, ed. Laurits Bødker, 127–
                45. Copenhagen: Rosenkilde and Bagger.
Tedlock, Dennis
1983   *The Spoken Word and the Work of Interpretation*. Phil-
                adelphia: University of Pennsylvania Press.
1990   "From Voice and Ear to Hand and Eye." *JAF*
                103:133–56.
Thompson, Stith
1955–1958   *The Motif-Index of Folk-Literature*, 6 Vols. Blooming-
                ton: Indiana University Press.
1965   "The Star Husband Tale." In *The Study of Folklore*, ed.
                Alan Dundes, 414–74.
Thompson, Stith, ed. and trans.
1973   *The Types of the Folktale*. FFC 184. Helsinki: Suoma-
                lainen tiedeakatemia (expanded edition of Antti
                Aarne's *Verzeichnis*).
Toelken, Barre
1979   *The Dynamics of Folklore*. Boston: Houghton Mifflin.
Turner, Victor
1967   "Themes in the Symbolism of Ndembu Hunting Rit-
                ual." In *Myth and Cosmos: Readings in Mythology and
                Symbolism*, ed. John Middleton, 249–69. Garden City:
                The Natural History Press, 1969.
1969   *The Ritual Process*. Ithaca: Cornell University Press.
Urbrock, William J.
1972   "Formula and Theme in the Song-Cycle of Job." In
                SBL 1972 Proceedings, Vol. 2, ed. Lane C. McGaughy,
                459–87. Missoula: Scholars Press.
1975   "Evidences of Oral-Formulaic Composition in the Po-
                etry of Job." Ph.D. Dissertation, Harvard University.
1976   "Oral Antecedents to Job: A Survey of Formulas and
                Formulaic Systems." *Semeia* 5:111–37.
Van Leeuwen, Raymond C.
1988   *Context and Meaning in Proverbs 25–27*. SBL Disserta-
                tion Series 96. Atlanta: Scholars Press.
Van Seters, John
1975   *Abraham in History and Tradition*. New Haven: Yale
                University Press.
1976   "Oral Patterns or Literary Conventions in Biblical Nar-
                rative." *Semeia* 5:139–54.

Vansina, Jan
1965   *Oral Tradition: A Study in Historical Methodology.* Chicago: Aldine.
1985   *Oral Tradition as History.* Madison: University of Wisconsin Press.

Westermann, Claus
1984/85/86 *Genesis. A Commentary.* 3 Vols. Minneapolis: Augsburg.

Whallon, William
1963   "Formulaic Poetry in the Old Testament." *Comparative Literature* 15:1–14.
1969   *Formula, Character, and Context.* Publications of the Center for Hellenic Studies. Cambridge: Harvard University Press.

Whitaker, Richard E.
1969   "A Formulaic Analysis of Uagritic Poetry." Ph.D. Dissertation, Harvard University.

Whybray, Roger N.
1989   "The Social World of Wisdom Writers." In *The World of Ancient Israel: Sociological, Anthropological, and Political Perspectives,* ed. Ronald G. Clements, 227–50. Cambridge: Cambridge University Press.

Widengren, Geo.
1948   *Literary and Psychological Aspects of the Hebrew Prophets.* Uppsala Universitets Arsskrift 10. Uppsala: Lundequist.
1959   "Oral Tradition and Written Literature among the Hebrews in the Light of Arabic Evidence, in Special Regard to Prose Narratives." *Acta Orientalia* 23:201–63.

Wilbert, Johannes and Karin Simoneau
1978   *Folk Literature of the Gê Indians,* Vol. 1. Los Angeles: UCLA Latin American Center Publications.
1983   *Folk Literature of the Bororo Indians.* Los Angeles: UCLA Latin American Center Publications.
1984   *Folk Literature of the Gê Indians.* Vol. 2. Los Angeles: UCLA Latin American Publications.

Wilson, Robert R.
1977   *Genealogy and History in the Biblical World.* New Haven: Yale University Press.
1980   *Prophecy and Society in Ancient Israel.* Philadelphia: Fortress.

Yocum, Margaret R.
1985   "Woman to Woman: Fieldwork and the Private Sphere." In *Women's Folklore, Women's Culture,* ed. Jordan and Kalcîk, 45–53.

Yoder, P. B.
  1970   "Fixed Word Pairs and the Composition of Hebrew Po-
              etry." Ph.D. Dissertation, University of Pennsylvania.
  1971   "A-B Pairs and Oral Composition in Hebrew Poetry."
              VT 21:470–89.
Zakovitch, Yair
  1981   "From Oral to Written Tale in the Bible" (in Hebrew).
              Jerusalem Studies in Jewish Folklore 1:9–43.
  1991   "Review of *Underdogs and Tricksters: A Prelude to Bib-
              lical Folklore.*" *JAF* 104:233–35.
Zimmerli, Walther
  1979   *Ezekiel 1: A Commentary on the Book of the Prophet
              Ezekiel, Chapters 1–24.* Hermeneia. Philadelphia: For-
              tress.
Zipes, Jack
  1983a   *Fairy Tales and the Art of Subversion.* New York:
              Widman.
  1983b   *The Trials and Tribulations of Little Red Riding Hood.*
              South Hadley, MA: Bergin and Garvey.
  1986   *Don't Bet on the Prince: Contemporary Feminist Fairy
              Tales in North America and England.* New York:
              Methuen.
  1988   *The Brothers Grimm.* New York: Routledge, Chapman,
              and Hall.

Scripture Index

Subject and Author Index